I Found my Destiny

by *Ulf Ekman*

The story of Ulf Ekman
and Word of Life, Sweden

Word of Life Publications

I FOUND MY DESTINY
Second edition, 1999

ISBN 91 7866 394 6

Printed in Finland by WSOY

Acknowledgments

Table Of Contents

Dedication

*I dedicate this book to all the
wonderful church members
of Word of Life in Uppsala,
whom the Lord Jesus has granted me
the great joy and privilege of serving
as their pastor and shepherd.
I love you and thank God for you!*

Introduction

Writing this book about Livets Ord (Word of Life) church in Sweden has been both exciting and difficult. Exciting because so much has happened. Difficult because it has all happened in such a short time.

Word of Life can be viewed from many angles. There are a lot of stories to tell. There has been great joy, but also trials and disappointments. Everything God does, he does through imperfect people. People have their limitations; their treasure is in jars of clay, and it is about the treasure that I want to write.

Many opinions are held about Word of Life. We who work there know we are not perfect. However, we also know that God has called us. The question is not whether we do a perfect job, but whether Word of Life is a work that God has raised up. I believe it is, and I hope that the story of the vision and work at Word of Life church will strengthen and inspire you to believe in him.

Jesus says in Mark's gospel 9:23: *"All things are possible to him who believes."* There is no limit to what God can do for and through you when you heed his voice and trust him.

In Christm

Ulf Ekman

CHAPTER ONE

Born Again—in Gothenburg

"Hallelujah!"

The handset almost reverberated as my friend shouted through the phone. He'd just put some vital questions to me to which I'd answered "Yes." His questions went something like:

"Do you believe in Jesus in your heart?"

"Are you prepared to state with your own mouth that Jesus is your Lord?"

"Are you honestly prepared to belong to him and follow him?"

"Have you given your life to him?"

He'd read several verses from the Bible to me and I'd openly acknowledged to him and before God that I now believed in Jesus. The "hallelujah" through the phone was almost disconcerting. It was only my friend Axel talking, but there was someone else more authoritative behind his voice, asking me if I was prepared to belong to Him and follow Him.

Here I sat, a complete novice, ignorant of the first thing about the Christian life, yet with a peace and assurance I'd never known before. I'd been saved, not just 'accepted Christianity as my religion', but saved and born again. I who'd felt disgusted at the very word "saved" and sneered at my own class-mates who read the Bible and believed in Jesus. What had happened?

My childhood in Gothenburg on Sweden's west coast during the 50s and 60s was nothing out of the ordinary. Ours was a stable working class home. There was no quarrelling, alcohol problem or lack of love. Only happy memories arise whenever I recall those days.

When I came home from school, my mother was always there, happy and cheerful. My father was a line maintenance man with Gothenburg Trams. He came home punctually from work, put his uniform cap complete with large badge on the hat shelf, washed his hands and sat down to a meal. After eating, he disappeared into the garage, showing up later to watch the 9 o'clock news on TV. My father wasn't specially talkative, but he read much and always represented steadfastness and security to me.

We didn't subscribe to an evening newspaper. We only read the *Gothenburg Post* and *The Work* which my father subscribed to through the union. Other than that we read the *Reader's Digest* and the *Council Worker,* a family weekly. Most of what we read was the best of left-wing thinking, and to vote for any other party than the Social Democrats was unthinkable for anyone in our home.

From the mid-60s and onwards, Swedish society started to become thoroughly radicalized. Even my

10

school in Gothenburg did not escape the influence, the dependable atmosphere changed into something drab that inspired rebellion.

It was during my high-school days that the national white-collar unions strike broke out, and we students took the special train to Stockholm to join in the protest march.

The Vietnam war began to cast its shadow over Sweden in those days too, and demonstrations increased. Numbers of fresh-green flower-power hippies, swaying to the sounds of The Beatles and Rolling Stones, suddenly blossomed into bright red radicals. They dreamed of the great revolution that would sweep away all the world's problems. A Chinese propaganda ship bristling with culture-revolutionists and spangled with blood-red catch phrases turned up in Gothenburg harbour. As for me, I bicycled from my home in the suburbs to the Marxist bookshop downtown to get hold of a copy of Mao's Little Red Book.

May-Day celebrations replaced the Mods riots, but only a few dedicated people mustered the enthusiasm to attend the "red classes" now being offered everywhere. Most of the young people found their way instead to the civic center at Aveny 18 or the many discos and parties being thrown around town.

Through the influence of the Beatles, interest in eastern religions had also been awakened by this time. Confusion was rampant. Should one choose outer revolution or inner mystery? One representative for the mystical choice, the Maharishi, repeatedly visited Sweden to introduce TM, Transcendental Meditation.

During my college years I turned these questions over and over in my mind. Contempt for all established order ran deep, the deepest of all being reserved for Christianity. It was in the midst of all these influences that I grew up.

Suddenly, one day a buddy of mine, Axel, got saved. It hit me like a thunderbolt. Whatever had happened? I knew that the poor fellow suffered from some sort of evangelical church background, but what was this? Gone, now, were our discussions about Wittgenstein, Herman Hesse, Buddhism and Socialism. All he talked about was Jesus!

Something in me was attracted. Something else made me miserable. He used to change ideologies like you change your jacket. But Axel, who tried most things, only to reject them shortly after, kept on talking about Jesus. I quickly withdrew and only saw him three or four times the following six months. But it was enough. I saw that he was changed. He was happier and definitely different and I began to feel uneasy, dirty, inconsistent and selfish.

In my third and final year at senior high school, a clergyman tought our religious education classes. Old Mr Ahlstedt relaxed behind the teacher's desk obviously enjoying every minute that he talked about Christianity. The more my classmates tried to shoot him down with their Marxist positions the more old Mr Ahlstedt seemed to enjoy himself. Responding calmly to their heated arguments, he said, "Christianity can be summed up in one word, 'joy'!"

I didn't know what to think. To me Christianity stood for everything that was dull, conservative, superstitious, oppressive and negative.The words of this old pastor were reassuring, calm, and free from conceit and deceit. He radiated with the things of which he spoke: peace and joy.

My disdain for the Bible was based entirely on sentiment. It was totally illogical. I who'd hardly ever opened a Bible—except at confirmation classes where I'd understood next to nothing—was still brazen enough to attack it. I bragged about having read the Upanishads and the Bhagavadghita, but knew nothing about Isaiah, Jeremiah, Paul or Peter. So when a Christian asked me what I had against the Bible, I fell painfully silent. My stupidity was exposed and I was embarrassed.

The life that my teacher described and the life that Axel lived spoke so clearly. It was hard to argue with them. What was worse, something was arguing from within me. My own conscience was beginning to be awakened. What I didn't know was that a group of Christians, among them, an American from the Jesus movement, were meeting to pray regularly that I would be saved. This opened the way for the Spirit of God to influence my heart through the Word that I was hearing from Axel and old Mr Ahlstedt.

One day, I skipped lessons and decided to bicycle to a church. It was closed, so I sat outside thinking. Finally, something gave way within me, exposing my pride and feeble attempts to run from God. When I got home, I called my friend, the one I'd done everything to avoid for the last six months, and asked him if I could come over and talk.

That Saturday night, May 28, 1970, I went over to Axel's place, my guard already up on arrival. No former buddy was going to get the better of me. We'd always had our debates, sometimes for hours over the 'phone, about the most idiotic ideas and problems. I'd no intention of letting him beat me now. When he asked if we might pray together, I almost boiled over. He'd already put on a Christian record about the 'tunnel of life' and every word was hitting me between the eyes. But I'd still rather have heard that song than hear Axel pray.

When he asked if he could pray for me I mumbled something about him being free to do whatever he liked. Axel began to pray aloud that I would be saved. As he did so, I began to feel sick. My conscience was smarting, while at the same time I became aware of a ferocious battle for my life in the very atmosphere of the room. It was later that I learned about warfare fought in the spiritual realm over people's souls. Didn't Jesus say in Mark 8:36 *"What good is it for a man to gain the whole world, yet lose his soul?"* Every individual's life is precious to God.

I could hold out no longer. Jumping up, I threw a hasty "goodbye" over my shoulder, rushed out of the apartment and took the train home. During the entire 45-minute journey, I could hear the words: "You can receive the forgiveness of sins!" inside. They rang through my mind all the way home.

When I got home, I fell silently to my knees in my room and asked Jesus to forgive me. Fumbling for words, I asked Him to come into my life and be my Lord. There and then I was born again. A peace that I'd never felt before settled upon my heart. It felt as though a huge stone had fallen from me.

The next morning, a Sunday, I awoke with my whole being flooded with peace. For the first time in years, I could feel I had a good conscience. I felt clean inside. Outside, I heard birds singing. Life felt completely new. It was new! I knew I was a Christian.

How I knew it, I had no idea at the time. I just knew it! Later I discovered in the Bible that John the apostle speaks about the assurance of salvation; *"I write these things to you who believe in the name of the Son of God so that you may know that you have eternal life"* (1 John 5:13).

My first thought as I got up was: "It's Sunday today. What do Christians do on Sundays? Why yes, they go to church. I must go to church." Off I went to the church where I was confirmed. It was a large, almost frightening gothic structure. Few people were attending the service. It felt strange to go inside and sit among several elderly ladies. My thoughts struggled inside me. "Get out of here!" something shouted, "this is no place for you." It was pride asserting itself again, but my hunger was stronger, and I stayed.

I do not know the name of the minister who took the service, but I'll thank him when I meet him in heaven. His sermon rescued me that day and reassured me of my salvation. First, he described a person who doesn't believe in God, unconverted, sinful, lost. Then he showed how the Spirit of God works on him, drawing him to Christ. He went on to explain how a person becomes a Christian, through the forgiveness of sins, on the grounds of what Jesus did on the cross when he took the sins of the world on himself. He then showed how we receive the gift of Christ by faith, through God's grace, and become new creatures in Christ Jesus, thus becomming a child of God.

I was stunned. The minister described in detail everything that had happened to me the evening before. I recognized every word of it personally, though I'd hardly opened the Bible and almost cheered aloud, "That's it, that's exactly what happened to me!" When the service was over, I prayed again, just to be on the safe side, that Jesus would really come into my life. On my way down the church steps, I knew there was no turning back. Now, I was a Christian!

Immediately, my life became filled with a deep longing. I thirsted for the Word of God like a thirsty person craves water. Life was different. Nature itself took on a special hue and my inner man was estatic with joy. Everything around me actually remained the same, which caused my unstable emotions to go up and down like a roller-coaster and my thoughts to fly everywhere.

Axel's "hallelujah" came just at the right time. I needed to confess my faith with my mouth, not only believe it with my heart. More help was on the way too. Doors to other Christians now began to open and reveal to me a whole new arena of prayer, Bible reading, fellowship, friends, evangelism, encouragement and support.

Just before being saved I had met Ray Durr, an American, who had been saved in the Jesus revival in USA. Axel had introduced him to me and he'd witnessed gently, but firmly and purposefully to me. Ray had made me feel terribly uncomfortable. If there was anyone I knew was right, it was Ray. He radiated Jesus. I was greatly attracted by what this man had. Though somewhat disconcerted by this, I still wanted to see him again.

Now, that I'd confessed Jesus as my Lord, Axel phoned to tell me that a group of friends was going to a tent meeting and asked would I like to come. In addition, the Chorals choir was scheduled to sing. The Chorals had sung at Aveny 18 six months earlier and I'd been deeply impressed. They'd been like a blinding flash of light in my thick spiritual darkness. Ray was also going to be at the tent. When I heard this, I wanted to go. I wanted to tell that gentle man that I was now a Christian too.

I'll never forget that meeting. We arrived a little late and the service had already started. The tent was full of people. The smell of the sawdust covering the floor filled the air and everyone was happy. The message was inspiring and dynamic. Every word was for me.

Ray was waiting for me and had saved me a seat. We caught sight of each other at the same time. God's love shone from his eyes. He laughed, I laughed and we hugged each other without saying a word. We just knew that we knew. Jesus was real! I was forgiven! I was truly a child of God and in Christ I was a new creation! It was overwhelming, wonderful and natural all at the same time! Just like having come home.

Some time after I was saved, I saw a marvellous scripture for the first time. That word engraved itself deeply within me: *"If anyone is in Christ, he is a new creation; the old has gone, the new has come!"* (2 Cor 5:17). I well remember my first reaction to this verse. It was, "Yes, that's right, I know, it's happened to me!" It wasn't that that verse, or any other verse told me how to think and react as a Christian. It happened the other way round. The Scriptures would confirm what I already knew in my heart to be true.

Genuine Christianity is just like old Mr Ahlstedt said: "Joy!" The joy of coming home, joy at finding

17

the way, joy at discovering something new, namely the kingdom of God, the joy of having my guilty conscience and fears relieved, joy over my new brothers and sisters, joy at who Jesus is and what he has done for me...

I have sometimes said that I was "saved almost against my own will" and, actually, I believe it's true. We say "I accepted Jesus," and from our side, that is correct. But from God's side it's different. The Bible says in Romans 3:10-11, *"There is no-one righteous, not even one; there is no-one who understands, no-one who seeks God."*

When I look back on my salvation and the life which now, praise God, is dead and buried, I see that it wasn't really I who sought God but God who sought me. Back in my Sunday school days I remember singing hymns about Jesus giving his life for the world. What an impression those songs made on me! I recall too, Grandma and Grandpa reciting evening devotions from the prayer book, loud and clear in their bedroom, while I lay on my bed in the next room listening.

After my confirmation, I remember how I attempted to read the Bible on my own, but also how I fled from God time after time. He gave me repeated opportunities to hear about Jesus, but I rebelled or ran. I now see that much of this so called "seeking" in philosophies, politics, other religions, music and experiences is not the heart's longing for God at all. It is merely people's totally rebellious, self seeking attempts and excuses to avoid him. My emptiness and the wounds I'd received were simply the results of my wilful desire to go my own way and an unwillingness to submit to God.

Had it not been for God's intervening grace and the influence of his Spirit on my will, I'd never have found Jesus. It was not I who sought and found him; it was he who sought and saved me. It was not I who approved and accepted his acts and teachings; it was he who, despite my actions and opinions, pardoned me and accepted me on the grounds of his redemption. Oh, what grace! Boundless grace! How indebted and grateful I am, that in spite of everything, I am accepted in the Beloved One!

Once I was saved, things started to happen to me in rapid succession. After some weeks, while I was still very up and down in my emotions and going through a grilling from my old classmates, I was baptized in the Spirit. Here is how it happened. Right after I had received the Lord Jesus, I knew I had to tell my old friends what had happened. No one told me "Now that you're a Christian you should tell others about it." I just felt that I had to "speak about what I had seen and heard."

Most of my friends could hardly believe it at first, then they quickly left me one after another. Taunts and sneers became an everyday occurance for me. One of my buddies, who'd always been tight-fisted, offered to buy me a beer. When I replied "No thanks" he swore and ran off. I met him downtown later that evening, drunk. Jeering, he reeled towards me saying "So you belong to 'the saved' bunch now, huh?" The hatred and spite pouring from him were so intense that my body shook and I felt nauseous. But when I replied, "Yes, I do!" he turned on his heels and ran away with his jeering friends.

Ray, who was with me, suggested that we go to his house and pray. We ran off. Once inside we talked for a few minutes before he asked me, "Do you know anything about speaking in tongues?" I looked at him, opened my mouth to answer and out poured rivers of tongues from my inner man! In an instant, my entire being was flooded with a totally unexpected experience of what the Bible calls the "baptism with the Spirit" (Acts 1:8, 2:1-4).

The bliss that followed, and the joy and the presence of God that filled me are indescribable. For about two hours I could do nothing but praise God in other tongues. Wave after wave of cleansing, power and love rolled through me. I was shocked, startled, taken off guard, but oh, how wonderful it was! Jesus is the One who baptizes in the Holy Spirit and fire (Matt 3:11), and I believe that at that moment, he severed many harmful links with my past, healed my wounds and filled me with His presence and glory.

Since then, I have never felt the slightest attraction to the old life again. God's power swept it completely out of my life. That isn't to say that as believers we aren't tempted. On the contrary, the struggle can sometimes be intense and every Christian still lives in his "flesh," irregardless of how many spiritual experiences he claims to have had. But the baptism in the Spirit supplies something no human ability can replace. It grants true supernatural power for what Jesus is calling us to do for Him, and with Him.

I would like to mention two more signifcant incidents from my past in Gothenburg. One of them took place on a train. While sitting there, a sudden thought, "There is no God!" invaded my mind. For a moment, I was dazed. Everything went black within me and the atmosphere around me chilled. But just as quickly, a response rosed up from within me, "Oh yes there is! There is a God!" I deliberately affirmed the thought and something extraordinary happened. I felt how a 'trap door' was opened in the back of my head and I sensed, or perceived, or saw in the spirit, a light shining from heaven right through the open door, into my mind and down into my heart. It was filled with a brilliant Presence. Since that experience, I have never doubted the existence of God again, not for one second. All loneliness, real or imagined, vanished then and there, and I've never felt lonely again, not for a single day of my Christian life.

Every day I sense the presence of Jesus through the Holy Spirit. In the ordinary things of life, in times of fatigue, of attack, of sin or worldliness, this blessed presence of Jesus has remained, and I've never felt alone since. I didn't understand it at the time, but now I see how vital it has been to me. There have been many opportunities to feel alone, isolated and despised, but it has never really gone very deep. Jesus says in John 14:15-17: *"If you love me, you will obey what I command. And I will ask the Father, and he will give you another Counsellor to be with you for ever, the Spirit of Truth. The world cannot accept him, because it neither sees him nor knows him. But you know him, for he lives with you and will be in you."*

The other incident took place as I was getting off a train. By this time I'd lost nearly all my friends and I was feeling a little bewildered and downhearted.

I'd taken an extra job as a longshoreman at the docks. One day as I stepped off the train at the Gothenburg freeport, the reality of the "Great Commission" suddenly dawned upon me. The words in Matt 28:18-20 that had been impressed upon me during confirmation classes now returned in full force.

Jesus said: *"All authority in heaven and on earth has been given to me. Therefore go and make disciples of all nations, baptizing them in the name of the Father and of the Son and of the Holy Spirit, and teaching them to obey everything I have commanded you. And surely I am with you always, to the very end of the age."*

The drab environment of the freeport along with my questions about my old friends faded away as every word in that passage flashed before the eyes of my inner man. I suddenly knew the path my life was going to take: to testify of Jesus, to train up disciples, to go into all the world, knowing that Jesus would be with me. It was only later that I realized that there, at that dingy train stop, the Lord showed me my entire future and what was to become my life's work. But in what way it would happen, I had no idea.

Never had I seen the city of Gothenburg look so beautiful! This was the city of my childhood and troublesome teen years, and finally the place of my new birth. But now I was to leave it. I thought I'd be away for only a short time, but later I realized that I was never to move back again.

The year before I had decided to attend the university in Uppsala. By a whim or fancy, I chose a course in ethnography, a study of non-western cultures, which was only offered at Uppsala at the time. Many of my friends wanted to study at Lund University in south Sweden, but I needed to break out and do something different, that's why I chose Uppsala. At the time I knew nothing of how God had his hand in all of this.

Summer passed quickly, but before it was time to leave for Uppsala, I accompanied a group of Christian friends to a camp in the countryside. Joining in that weeks Bible study was wonderful to me. I was newly saved and hardly knew that the book of Habakkuk existed, nor had I read the Song of Solomon and heard about the Bridegroom's love for his bride.

The first night, a blind evangelist who had the gifts of healing was preaching. Well into the meeting, he paused and said, "There's someone here who has a problem with his left kidney." As he said it, the power of God shot through my body. I shook like a leaf. The person sitting beside me said, "Hey, that must be you! I can see it. He wants you to go to the front!" I went forward and told the people how Jesus had healed me. For a whole year I'd suffered from sharp pains in the side but I'd not let my parents know nor did I seek a doctor's help. However, from that moment on, all pain and discomfort in my side left permanently, and I discovered that this same Jesus who saves sinners and baptizes in the Holy Spirit, also heals the sick.

The week was over and it was time for water baptism. I was baptized in a little river nearby and it was a wonderful feeling to go down into that water knowing I was coming up again into a new life with Jesus. (Rom 6:4)

When I look back, I see how God used many different members in the Body of Christ to help me develop in the faith. These things spell out an unmistakable message to me; Jesus will never allow himself to be tied down to one system. He is present wherever people believe in him and expect things from him.

It is impossible to describe all my impressions and my amazement at God's goodness in the experiences I had during those early days, and as I set out for Uppsala, I had no idea what awaited me there...

CHAPTER TWO

Preparation—in Uppsala

It was stimulating to come to Uppsala. Life was exhilarating. My memories of it are pleasant. In high school my appetite for study had been sporadic because of an undisciplined, non-Christian lifestyle. Now, things were different. My hunger for learning began to stir. The desire to study that lay dormant in me began to grow.

Uppsala is a grand city, and an educational center. But to experience it you must throw yourself into its academic environment. For those who crave for knowledge, this is the place to be.

In Gothenburg I'd met Christians who both knew their Bible and were also specially good at testifying of their faith. I was fascinated to watch them look up passage after passage about Jesus and Paul and quote, compare and converse freely, sometimes long into the night. I longed to do the same, but at that time it seemed impossible.

Even before I was saved, I'd tried to understand the Bible, but couldn't. Once I was reading it at random. Romans 13 came up: *"Everyone must submit*

*himself to the governing authorities, for there is no
authority except that which God has established. The
authorities that exist have been established by God."* To
my shame I remember how I threw the Bible at the
wall, accusing Paul of "capitalistic nonsense."

Now, in Uppsala, I so craved the Word of God that I
could allow this scripure to work in me and put me
straight. On only the second day in the city, during
registration, I met some Christians who ran
café-evangelism in the basement under the main
auditorium of the University. They invited me to a
Bible study and I went right away. The group came
from different Christian backgrounds but they all
belonged to the student organization called the Navigators, for which I will always thank God. Meeting
the Navigators has made a permanent impression on
my life.

Three things characterized this organization: evangelism, scripture memorization and discipleship
training. The same things I'd seen among my friends
in Gothenburg I longed for. My young spiritual life
had consisted largely of dramatic experiences. I'm
sure I would not have been saved otherwise. However, what Jesus said in Matthew 7:24 about the wise
man who *"built his house on the rock"* I knew little
about. I needed a foundation and stability, and I was
about to receive it.

To enter that disciplined, Bible-study environment
where God's Word was central—preached then prac-
ticed—was revolutionary to me. At first glance these
students seemed a bit square but again I had to humble myself. They loved Jesus, they knew the Word of
God and they evangelized practically every day. I was
careless and undisciplined. An ongoing process now

began without which I probably wouldn't be a Christian today.

I'll never forget the day when the leader asked us to come a little dressed up because we were going out witnessing. I came in dirty shoes. He smiled, bent down and brushed them while I watched, embarrassed. One could not misinterpret his love.

Activities now began to increase: Bible studies, scripture memorization, orientation studies for unsaved students, door-knocking, friendship-evangelism, Bible study conferences etc. Every free moment that I had after my university studies, which now included ethnography, history and religious science, went to the Navigators. And I don't regret it for a minute.

My first three years in Uppsala, while obtaining a bachelor's degree in philosophy, were spent intensively in this way. Moving from one college residential area to another to evangelize, we ran meetings for law students, medical students and others. We worked-out at gyms with non-Christian undergraduates and were constantly out talking with fellow students about Jesus. It was wonderful, while together, we enjoyed close and inspiring fellowship.

After a time, two of us moved in with the leader of the student work in Uppsala. Darrel, an American with a Calvinistic background, had a love for the Word of God that was exceptionally evident. Several local leaders met on Saturday mornings at 7 a.m. to study Romans verse by verse and we went through the epistle studying it in-depth, never using commentaries, only different translations and dictionaries. It took us a year to get through Romans in this way, covering half a chapter a week. Two evenings were set aside for preparatory studies and then we'd meet on Saturday mornings to share our findings. Those occasions in the Word of God were precious, and I'll never forget them. Getting into the habit of learning the Word of God by heart was a great exercise for my mind. We learned hundreds of scriptures, verse by verse, encouraging each other all the time. While we were going through Romans (which we did twice), we learned whole chapters by heart. I would bicycle through the city park to Carolina Rediviva, the university library. On the way there in the mornings I would recite two chapters, and two more on my way home in the evening. I worked my way through the whole epistle that way.

It might sound extreme, but for me it was extremely wholesome and extremely enjoyable. The whole procedure resembled a spiritual boot-camp, and I am deeply grateful for the privilege of having gone through it. Sitting in my dormitory room one Saturday evening, enjoying studying Romans with paper, pen, Bibles and dictionaries spread open on the table, I heard a knock at the door. Some fellow students came in to ask me a favor. They were going to a party and wanted me to give them a wake-up call in the morning. When they saw the Bibles open on my table they went quiet, wondering what I was doing. I recall how happy I was, to explain what I was busy doing. They were astonished! The presence of God so filled the room they stood open-mouthed. I suppose they'd never seen anything like it before.

I spoke to my dormitory mates several times about Jesus. One of them put up a big poster of Mao on his door. His door was opposite mine. I put an equally large one up with the words: "What will it profit a man if he gains the whole world and forfeits his own soul?" Every morning as he left for lectures, he saw those words.

Student evangelism was inspiring. Every week, sometimes several days a week, we were out on campus or at home having Bible studies for hungry seekers. During that time we met an astonishing number of many kinds of people, and had countless conversations with them about Jesus. Still today, it's amazing to recall how non-believing students would sit, week after week, studying John's gospel chapter by chapter and asking questions on the content!

Those experiences of "grass-roots evangelism" were invaluable. There are so many Christians who have never had the excitement of inviting non-believing neighbors in to study the Word of God and leading them to the Lord. What a joy it was when a student would bow his heart and receive Jesus after a time of Bible study. I sensed how my room lit up and the peace of God came flooding in at such times.

While all this was going on in my life, out of public view, the Charismatic revival came to Sweden. During almost all of my time with the Navigators from 1970 to 1975, I remained outside of that revival. The revival presented no problem to me, but the Navigators, as a movement, had little sympathy for the baptism and gifts of the Spirit. I was already baptized in the Spirit, but was instructed by them to speak in tongues at home "in the closet" and nowhere else. As a newborn Christian I had little knowledge of what was right or wrong, knowing only that the Lord wanted me to be in the "Navs" and to be thoroughly grounded in his word. So I prayed in tongues sporadically and only when alone.

Following my bachelor's degree, I started studying theology full time. A hunger had been awakened in me for exhaustive Bible study and I wanted to be able to read the New Testament in Greek. It was in this context that I read a book, The Rock Solid Foundation, by a Swedish clergyman. It gripped me deeply, and it was while I was reading it, that the idea of studying for the ministry began to take form.

People from every denomination joined the Navigators and we used to visit different evangelical churches on Sundays. At the time, I was a member in a pleasant little church that had an inspiring pastor who preached excellent sermons. Little by little, however, I felt the call to the ministry and to study for my ordination. However, there were some theological hurdles such as baptism to clear on the way. I was hungry for knowledge, and God was leading me unmistakably along this path.

After the introductory course, I began to react to the liberal theology being spread out as truth. This continued until I took the Bachelor of Theology examination. Reading theology was stimulating and useful, but the slothfulness, worldliness, unbelief and lukewarmness I met in my fellow students was incredible. It is not my purpose to judge the Institute of Theology at Uppsala. There, many fine lectures have been given and many good students have graduated, but the spiritual life in the 70s was deplorable.

Bible believing students didn't have an easy time. The systematic demolishing of their "simple faith" was grievously effective. I remember a lecturer in Old Testament studies who said off-handedly, "You might as well glance through the Pentateuch some time—as a curio." As a mere curio! Here I was, reading through them at least once a year in my Bible study plan and memorizing verses from them!

There was never any prayer before lessons and no belief in the supernatural. Unbelief was rampant, and the lecturers themselves were often incredibly scornful. Yet I enjoyed being there. I knew it was where I should be, and that was enough. One of our lecturers told us, "You must learn to be critical" and I thought, "You're right, and I'll begin by questioning you!"

What was most tragic however was seeing students, confident in faith, turn in a few months into hesitant agnostics or sceptics and some into confirmed unbelievers. Perhaps their teachers thought they were doing their students a service, training them to become more mature and 'discerning.' For some of them, however, the lectures were sheer seduction and a tragedy.

If anything stirred up my fighting spirit against liberal, unbelieving theology, it was my studies at the Theological faculty of Uppsala university. Naturally, the debate about the authenticity of the Bible as the Word of God drew me in too. I said to the Lord repeatedly, "If this is your opinion of the Bible, I'm willing to change my opinion." Every time I prayed that prayer, the Lord answered me from the Scriptures, confirming and strengthening me in my conviction that the Bible was truly the inspired Word of God, fully adequate for man's salvation, and that we

---

* The five books of Moses

have it today in the form that God wants it to be, and that it is reliable in all it says.

This is not to say that the Bible does not contain mysteries, or difficult passages. However, for those who've come to know the Author, it is easy to have confidence in what he says. If anyone is hungry for bread, you don't give him a stone; if someone wants an egg, you don't hand him a scorpion. But here were many students, breaking their teeth on stones and being handed scorpions instead of being encouraged to honestly investigate the Word of God.

Just as I did with the Navigators, I met Christians from a rich variety of backgrounds here. There were Catholics, people from high- and low-church backgrounds and Lutherans side by side with old-fashioned pietists and evangelicals of varying persuasions. You could choose to attend anything from canticles in the cathedral to charismatic prayer meetings in someone's kitchen. You could discuss Luther with the most old-fashioned pietist or debate liberalism with wine-bibbing revolutionary Christian socialists. You would meet would-be-clergymen who weren't interested in the Bible for a minute and believers who prayed and fasted for days for the nation. There were those who crossed themselves, inflected, walked backwards out of church and argued the significance of incense, and tongues-talking theologians who prayed for the sick and cast out demons. Spiritual life was, to say the least, multi-faceted, and sometimes, confusion seemed to reign supreme.

One day one of the chaplains asked if I might like to accompany him on a retreat on the subject of "The Holy Spirit" just outside Uppsala. Half reluctantly I went, sensing that the Lord might be telling me to go, but after a day and a half, I wondered what I was doing there. I felt heavy and considered going home.

Time came for the evening Bible study and we sat in a circle while the priest droned on uninspiringly. To this day I can't remember what he talked about, but right across from me sat a redheaded girl. I couldn't take my eyes from her. Who was she I wondered? When the drowsy Bible study was finally over and everyone went out for a walk, the redhead and I found ourselves beside each other. That evening a relationship began that has only grown stronger and stronger through the years. God brought the person into my life who would affect and influence me more than anyone else.

Birgitta was wonderful! We truly discovered each other immediately. We shared common interests and began to see one another frequently. I was in love up to my ears—and I still am today! Like a fresh spring breeze, Birgitta came into my life and quickly became a vital part of my life... and since that time, our lives together have been an exciting adventure.

Having met, she told me about her background as a child of missionaries in India and that she was a widow and mother of a wonderful little son, Aron. My first meeting with Aron, who was six-and-a-half at the time, was unforgettable. When they arrived at my home, he skipped right into my arms as though we'd always known each other! Later, as they were leaving, he gave me a friendly smile and commented, "You're welcome to come over any time you like!" And I did.

Our wedding was in December 1976. It was a great privilege to adopt Aron. He became my wonderful son whom I love so much. He's always given me so much, and continues to give me more today. His words and advice have often helped me, though he'll hardly admit it.

Before we were married, Birgitta and I talked a lot about the things God was doing. She possessed a broad Christian background; her parents were Methodist missionaries and her youth was spent in the Lutheran church. She'd been active in the charismatic revival, and for a short time, in the Pentecostal church also. Through my friendship with Birgitta my praying in tongues revived. We prayed a lot together and the Lord refreshed me deeply. Often while we were talking about the Bible, she would say, "That's not what my dad says. He says..." I hadn't yet met my father-in-law-to-be, Sten Nilsson, and wondered why she quoted him so frequently.

On one occasion we started talking about healing. A bit off handed, I said that God puts sicknesses on people. "No he doesn't," objected Birgitta, "he heals them!" A little presumptuously I retaliated, "OK, let's look up the book of Job," We looked up Job 2:7 and I got a shock. I thought I knew the verse well, I could even recite it. But I hadn't seen what was written there: *"So Satan went out from the presence of the Lord and afflicted Job with painful sores from the soles of his feet to the top of his head."* It was the Accuser who'd afflicted Job! And I'd never seen it before. Nor had I seen what was written in Luke 13:16: *"should not this woman, a daughter of Abraham, whom Satan has kept bound for eighteen long years, be set free on the Sabbath day from what bound her?"*

I'd read the verse several times but not noticed that it was Satan who'd kept the woman bound and that she, a daughter of Abraham and co-heiress of the covenant, had a right to the healing that Jesus gave her. Neither had I ever reflected on what I'd read in Acts 10:38. Now, it hit me like a thunderbolt, *"...how God anointed Jesus of Nazareth with the Holy Spirit and power, and how he went around doing good and healing all who were under the power of the devil, because God was with him."* It was then I realized that there was a lot I didn't know, especially concerning healing, the power of God and the supernatural life in Christ.

To meet Sten Nilsson was, and still is, fascinating. He is a wonderfully kind man of God who is humble while bold, and caring and yet carefree. It was glorious to come into this loving, open-hearted missionary home through meeting Birgitta. They often talked about the land they love, India. Birgitta could speak for a long time about the villages in Santal Parganas, the mission station in Theodori and the school situated high in the Kodaikanal mountains in the south.

Sten enjoyed retelling his mission adventures, but he'd relish even more describing the interdenominational Ashram meetings in Sweden where prayer was made for the sick and the miracle healings that followed. In the same way that I, as a fresh believer, had felt an insatiable thirst for God's word, I now found a unquenchable thirst for the supernatural life described in the Bible. I suddenly noticed God doing wonders and miracles wherever I read and I began to wonder how I'd missed it before; I who'd read the Bible day in and day out.

I can recall Bible studies with the Navigators where we studied Mark's gospel all day long for days. Each day we brought out the principle of Jesus training His disciples. They were stimulating days, but not once did anyone mention the fact that Jesus, particularly in Mark's gospel, constantly healed the sick and instructed His disciples to do the same. In the Great Commission in Mark's gospel 16:17-20 He commanded His disciples to speak in tongues, cast out devils and lay hands on the sick so that they would recover. It goes on to say how He worked with them when they went out to preach by confirming His Word with accompanying signs and wonders.

It was as though this entire side of God's word had remained hidden from me. Why? For one thing, I'd been in circles where there was no expectation or faith for the supernatural manifestations which are an integral part of the gospel. I can recall how people on various occasions explained away whole sections of scripture about healing, miraculous signs and wonders. It was as though some Christians said, "Yes, but not here and now", or "No, that was added later, it's an exaggeration and a legend."

Many believers were really agnostics when one talked about the gospel as "God's power." Either theological glasses or lack of expectation among Christian leaders blunted the entire sense of some scriptures causing stunted growth of believers.

To me, a whole new glorious arena opened up. The Bible was like new! Jesus' healing ministry fascinated and challenged me. One day, I received some audio cassette tapes from my father-in-law. They came from an American Bible teacher named Kenneth Copeland. I'll never forget them. They were recordings of radio bible studies on subjects like the authority we have in Jesus' name, based on

1 John 3:23. *"And this is His commandment, that we should believe on the name of His Son Jesus Christ, and love one another, as He gave commandment."*

He taught on subjects like faith in the name of Jesus, understanding the power and authority in his name, what faith is, how it comes, what it can do, seeing the possibilities it opens up, realizing that it can cast mountains into the sea, that nothing is impossible through faith in Jesus and that it overcomes the world—all this was awesome! When I listened to those tapes, it was as though every verse and passage of Scripture I had memorized suddenly exploded. The unction of the Holy Spirit taught me the meaning of so many passages which had lain dormant in my mind. Suddenly I saw and grasped things I'd never seen before!

The life and ministry of Jesus, the ministry of each believer, the supernatural life in Christ Jesus became brilliantly clear as never before. I've never known such a spiritual hunger as during the time that followed. Birgitta and I listened to tapes as often as we could. Night after night we had our own 'Bible school' and received so much new revelation. I phoned my friend, Robert Ekh. Soon he was sitting on a chair in our kitchen listening to a tape while the Word of God went right into him and transformed his life. A tremendous time of Bible studies, prayer groups, and theological studies followed.

Soon, the period of time arrived in my university studies which was to be devoted to research on a specific subject. All that term I studied healing. Day by day I sat in the university library reading the Bible and going through books on the subject. As a result, faith for miracles, signs and wonders, healing and deliverance grew all the stronger within me. Our tutor, associate professor Sigbert Axelsson, wasn't overjoyed with the results, but faith grew mightily and unabatingly in me.

I fail to see that healing, God's power, and the manifestation of the Spirit along with signs and wonders are granted to only some particular denomination or movement. Throughout the history of the church, nearly every new revival or rediscovered spiritual truth has been branded as "extreme" or "sectarian". Frequently, the revelation and blessing the Lord wanted to impart to his church was despised and criticized, and because it wasn't received, it actually did become exaggerated or extreme.

People's reluctance to change their theological eye glasses or their unwillingness to see that their knowledge is incomplete, has caused them to miss God given experiences of things they possessed in Christ, simply because of some narrow-minded idea they hold which they think is purely divine but is mostly human. These experiences do belong to them because the Bible speaks of them, making them an integral part of the gospel and the work of the Spirit. The Holy Spirit wants to make all these things living and real to every believer by experience.

In the early church, it was not as though one little group of people had a monopoly on the baptism in the Spirit, another group had divine healing, others had teaching and the rest had communion. All participated in everything. This is why the rediscovery of ancient biblical truth does not imply a change of denomination or movement. For practical reasons, this may occur if a church or denomination closes its doors to the Word of God. But this is not God's best.

As my studies in theology began to draw to a close, I prayed to the Lord concerning the future. I could not easily visualize myself as a minister in a rural parish. During the summers, under permit from the priest, I had preached in the diocese of Gothenburg and the cathedral parish of Uppsala. Now I prefered to continue evangelizing among students and holding Bible studies.

Sweden's Evangelical Student Movement, SESG, needed a chaplain and I was asked to consider it. It came completely unexpectedly. I'd had no previous contact with them and I'd heard that they rarely recruited helpers outside their own ranks in the evangelical Lutheran church. As I prayed to the Lord, I felt that I should really put this to the test to see if it was from Him by declining the offer. If this was from God, they would come back again. I declined. Others were interested in the position, but I was asked again. This time I got a scripture from the Lord with an assurance that it was His will; so I said "yes". The scripture was Ezekiel 2:1-3, where God sends the prophet to a backslidden Israel, to prophesy to them whether they would listen or not, and to be unafraid of their words. It was a suitable passage for the university environment where I would work, and it would be repeated later on another, very special occasion.

We had now come to the final "crowning" term at the university which included our "priestly-practicals" before the ordination. On one occasion, it was announced that a professor, accompanied by so-called Christian homosexuals, would talk to all would-be-priests in order to "increase their tolerance" towards such people. This would be the first of three confrontations with this professor. A group of us students got together in prayer and bound the spirit behind the impending seduction.

The day came and the professor seemed a bit jittery. When his propaganda was finished, it was time for questions. I sat quietly praying in tongues until I felt God say, "Now!" I requested to speak and asked the professor what he thought about Romans 1:27 *"In the same way, the men also abandoned natural relations with women and were inflamed with lust for one another. Men committed indecent acts with other men, and received in themselves the due penalty for their perversion."*

The professor, usually highly cultivated and correct and the very picture of politeness, became very much annoyed. According to him the whole discussion now took the wrong turn and he publicly stated that anyone with such views as mine was unsuitable for the priesthood. The meeting finished in tumult, but at the least his perverted views on homosexuality gained no victory.

Later, when I had become chaplain, the professor returned and tried to interrupt a Bible study which I was holding. It was entitled, "God's view of sexuality." This time he had no success either. The student in charge of the meeting stood up and asked the professor to kindly be quiet during "divine service."

The last contact I had with him was when archbishop Bertil Werkström asked me to leave the priesthood. The professor in question desired to be in on the proceedings but I declined his request and the archbishop asked him to sit outside. This final meeting took place at a much later time. In the meantime a lot would happen...

CHAPTER THREE

The Adventure Begins—in Tulsa

On Sunday 28 January 1979 the bells of Gusta-vus Cathedral boomed out across the city of Gothenburg signalling an ordination. My father, who had nearly fallen off his chair when I first told him I was going to study for the clergy, had come round to the idea by now and was more nervous than I was. My whole family—Birgitta with Aron and our baby son Jonathan, a little over a year old—had come for the occasion.

Bishop Gärtner officiated at the awe-inspiring pro-ceedings. Afterwards, among the thronging clergy-men, I bumped into an old vicar. He was among those who'd just laid their hands on me at the altar. I recog-nized him at once. Years ago, he'd been my Christian Education teacher in the seventh grade at school, and I hadn't seen him since. He had run a competi-tion in class once and I'd won it and had gone up to receive my prize—a little booklet on Christianity. Looking at me in a fatherly fashion, he'd admonished me in front of the others, "Maybe, Ulf, you should study for the clergy."

How embarrassed I'd been. I couldn't get back to my seat quick enough. Now, all these years later, I walk right into him at my ordination. How extraordinary!

Following my ordination, I served for a week in a church outside of Gothenburg where I had the privilege of an hour's conversation with the nationally-known elderly bishop, Giertz, and was able to tell him how much his books had meant to me. Directly after that, it was time for me to begin my work as a chaplain to the students in the university of Uppsala. The numbers attending the meetings rose steadily and we had to change our meeting place several times. First we met in the little Christian bookstore. From there we moved to the Church Mission rooms, and then to the spacious Humanities Center lecture theatre at the university. Increasing numbers of students looking for the truth visited our Bible studies and several came to the Lord. Some even received the baptism in the Holy Spirit, and healing, and deliverance.

Some of the things we did were a little difficult for a traditional, evangelical Lutheran movement like SESG to take. However, no critical conflicts broke out while I was there. There were tensions, but real conflicts arose only later—and then, for real.

Baptism in the Holy Spirit was one of the points of conflict. The expression "baptism in the Holy Spirit" was considered as appropriate for pentecostal denominations only and "here, we use the term, 'infilling' or 'fullness' of the Holy Spirit," they said. Healing was definitely controversial, especially in the form of Kenneth Hagin's books or teaching. My office was in the Christian Bookstore which at the time offered a great deal of books on liberal theology. When I removed them and replaced them with more biblical, though not always Lutheran, literature, there was even more reaction.

My hunger for God kept growing all this time. In March 1980, my father-in-law, Sten, helped me make a trip to Tulsa, Oklahoma in the U.S. to observe what God was doing there. I'd been reading and enjoying Hagin's books for some time by then. Now, I would be able to see what God was doing through Rhema Bible Training Center in Tulsa. The trip was of utmost importance for me. A friend and I travelled together—and what liberty and glory we experienced! Neither of us had much money over and above the tickets (which my father-in-law had bought) so we had to live there by faith. Every day became a supernatural walk of faith!

The church services were greatly uplifting and the spiritual freedom, astounding. People were being saved, healed and baptized in the Spirit in every meeting. We spent ten days in Tulsa listening to Kenneth Hagin and Lester Sumrall, who was visiting just then. Following that, we made a journey to a conference to hear Kenneth Copeland in Albequerque, New Mexico and finally made our way to John Osteen's church in Houston, Texas. What a world of difference we found compared with the setting from which we had come. No narrow sectarianism here. No intellectual unbelief, no negativism, no complaints, no suspicion, no antagonistic party-spirit, but a happy, positive expectation of powerful, spiritual manifestations from Jesus and the Holy Spirit. The supernatural Christian life was functioning as it should. God was doing miracles and we were able to listen to strong, faith-building Bible teaching. We also saw big churches growing even bigger. Everywhere we went we met loving people. In every place they laid hands on us, prayed for us and encouraged us with prophetic utterances.

In one of these meetings, Lester Sumrall preached. In the middle of his sermon he stopped, turned in our direction and declared, "There are people in this auditorium whom God will hold accountable for the lives of thousands of people, if they do not leave the dead circles in which they are involved today." As he spoke those words, looking right at us where we stood among the thousands of others, I felt the power of God go straight through me like a spiritual thunderbolt. I knew that God had spoken to me!

This does not mean that everything in the Swedish state church or evangelical churches was dead. Not at all! But to me, those words spelled out a spiritual move in which I would find greater freedom and really begin to do what I sensed the Lord had called me to do. In my inner man I saw my clerical collar fly from my neck—like a seagull borne away on the wind!

In another of these meetings I had a vision. I have only had a few visions, and this was one of those occasions. While I watched, an acorn was planted in a wide expanse of open terrain in deep, rich soil. Up came a mighty oak to maturity, with branches spreading in every direction and forming a full

---

* Ekman means "Oakman" in Swedish.

crown. The image then changed, and I saw a fish lying on a rock at the side of the sea, gasping for breath, its gills flapping. Suddenly, it leaped into the air, splashed into the water, swam rapidly back and forth and in circles—rather like an aquarium fish released into its tank from a bag—and so it vanished out to sea. I then heard the Holy Spirit say, "Now I am placing you in your proper element, the SUPER-NATURAL."

These experiences had a revolutionary effect on me. When I came home, I wasn't just hungry for more of the supernatural side of the gospel and God's life, I had been indelibly stamped by it for ever. Returning home, I felt an anointing come upon me that I'd never sensed before. From that time on, after those experiences, the opposition began to stiffen.

Looking back on that time I am persuaded that the Lord was not talking to me about churches and organizations primarily. The Bible makes it clear that Christians can live in the Spirit or in the flesh, in obedience or in obstinacy, in the kingdom of God or in the world. I believe that the Lord was telling me, (and I hadn't fully understood it), to live a spiritual life which draws upon His supernatural resources and not a life of human limitations and traditions and this world's values. The dividing line between these two does not run between the different denominations.

For example, Pentecostal Christians do not automatically live in the spirit or hold a monopoly on doctrine, while members of other churches live in the flesh and are wrong on every point. No, in every setting, including what we today call the Faith Movement, people can live in the flesh or in the Spirit. A certain doctrine, a particular denomination, a special tradition, a singular liturgy or a special preacher are never sufficient to guarantee that we are right. Every day we are dependent on the grace of God. Every day we are dependent on Jesus. Every day we are called to be led by the Spirit of God. Every day, we who are justified are urged to live by faith.

The Body of Christ is more than just the official state church or the Pentecostal movement, a Faith church or a particular manifestation of the Holy Spirit. The Body of Christ is to be found wherever people confess Jesus as their Lord. It cannot be confined to one setting only. The Lord wants all believers, irrespective of church or background, to develop in him and to personally enjoy the life and liberty and the victory and benefits that Jesus died to give us, and which God's word plainly promises us.

After the trip to America, many things happened. One in particular: Birgitta and I were offered a post as missionaries in Bangladesh where we would start a work among students. At this point, something extraordinary happened. We received a divine prophecy, confirming that we should go, which was undoubtedly from God.

We accepted the offer, but both Birgitta and I became increasingly unsure about going. Should we then go? And if we shouldn't, was the prophecy from God or wasn't it? An explanation would come later.

At the same time, I was invited to preach at St. Ansgar's Chapel in Uppsala. St. Ansgar's was the very cornerstone of high church establishment among the students. Evangelical preachers of revival were seldom invited to minister there. However, a number of students pressed their request and I was called to preach at the Mass. Possibly, the invitation was a way of yielding to that pressure and easing some tension, which had arisen since many students who attended my bible studies also attended St. Ansgar's.

On the morning that I was to preach, the Lord spoke to my inner man saying, "You must prophesy." "Never!" I thought. But then the words of Ezekiel 2:4-5 rose within me: *"The people to whom I am sending you are obstinate and stubborn. Say to them, 'This is what the sovereign Lord says.' And whether they listen or fail to listen—for they are a rebellious house—they will know that a prophet has been among them."*

I was terrified. All the way into town I was ready to jump out of the car. My entire inner man was quaking. Several priests officiated in the service, and while I sat there, clad in white cloak, vestment and all, awaiting my turn, my knees shook. Then came the time to preach my sermon. When I was finished, I took a deep breath, raised my right hand, closed my eyes and prophesied.

Once I was through, I was so relieved I could have turned cartwheels round the altar. Great joy and boldness came upon me. I felt I could do anything! Above all, however, I knew I had obeyed God. My message had been about unity and evangelism to reach the lost. If it was received, I do not know, but I know I sensed an overwhelming freedom afterwards.

As time wore on, my hesitation about the move to Bangladesh grew. One day, Birgitta and I talked about it. Neither of us felt joy or peace or any inner witness that it was right to go, despite the powerful prophecy we'd had and irregardless of the fact we'd said yes to the offer. As we prayed, another word arose within us. "Go to Tulsa and attend Rhema

Bible Training Center for a year." Instantly, our joy, our peace and our enthusiasm flooded back. It was glorious to have it, but that was all we had. If we should choose Bangladesh we would receive training, a guaranteed salary, traveling expenses, and perhaps even a cook and a servant. If, on the other hand, we went to Tulsa, nothing would be guaranteed. Not only were we without money, but we knew our decision to make the trip would meet fierce opposition from certain believers. There were other repercussions too, but we were finally released, and in August 1981 we set out for Rhema.

My work as a chaplain to the students was now over. 400 students had gathered for the final meeting. We had started with about 35 students. Much had happened in between. Many students had been spiritually renewed and when we left SESG we felt that our task there was completed. We'd had some differences and there had been some tensions, but no hard words were exchanged or reproaches given. My brothers and sisters in Christ there are fine Christians and even if we don't share the same persuasions on every point, I still look back on my time there as chaplain with joy. I learned a lot there and had many wonderful experiences with the Lord Jesus and with my brothers and sisters in him.

On the plane to the U.S. the man sitting in front of me opened a newspaper. Huge headlines across a double-page spread spelled out: THIS IS WHERE THE BIG ADVENTURE BEGINS! I don't know what the article was about but the title suited us well, for we were on the threshold of things more thrilling than we'd ever known before.

First of all, we were unsure if we'd get through customs. The enemy was hammering non-stop at my mind, nagging, "You won't even clear customs. You'll have to turn around and go home in disgrace and shame!" The reason for my doubts was that at that time, Rhema did not permit people to study at their school before applicants had been granted a student visa by the American embassy. Now the embassy did not approve applications to a non-registered school. Rhema was non-registered then. So we set off without any guarantees of even getting through customs.

Well, we got through, thanks to a vague letter of invitation to visit a church in Tulsa. It was written by Billy Joe Daugherty in Victory Christian Center. The second "thriller" came when we discovered that we had far too little money. What we had lasted a few months and then it was gone. In America they thought our finances were secured in Sweden. In Sweden, they thought we were getting help in the USA. We got neither.

A step at a time, the Lord performed financial miracles all the year through. It was a fantastic school-of-learning, seeing the Lord take care of us in every conceivable and inconceivable way. Our son Samuel had been born in July of 1980, and we were now a family with three boys. Sometimes, we didn't have a penny, or a dime. But we were able to pay our bills all through the year—and to practise our faith by trusting God day by day.

A scripture we stood on was Deuteronomy 8:7-9: *"The Lord your God is bringing you into a good land—a land with streams and pools of water, with springs flowing in the valleys and hills; a land with wheat and barley, vines and fig-trees, pomegranates, olive oil and honey, a land where bread will not be scarce and you will lack nothing; a land where the rocks are iron and you can dig copper out of the hills."*

If we didn't have money, we always had food. If there was no food, there was always a little money and some reduced-price coupon that could be used at a food store somewhere. We were given an old beat-up car, as big as a house and thirsty as a tanker but that got us everywhere. Sometimes we only had one dollar with which to "fill up" but it was always sufficient to get us to a meeting or prayer-group and then home again. Life was wonderful! To attend a real Bible school and listen to renowned, anointed teachers and preachers was wonderful. And to listen to faith teaching from Kenneth Hagin at the Bible school, the prayer-and-healing school and his special seminars were a sheer delight. Every day was special and every meeting a privilege. Birgitta and I enjoyed it fully. What grace to spend a whole year in this way in God's Word!

Several things made strong impressions upon us. First, of course, it was glorious to soak in the Word of God itself and not a theology that placed doubt on its accuracy or talked about everything else but the Word. Neither was it insignificant to be in a milieu where the Spirit of God was powerfully at work.

Second, it was glorious to be in a dynamic and fast-growing church. Victory Christian Center under pastor Billy Joe Daugherty was newly started and growing quickly all the time. There was a loving spirit in the church coupled with a robust faith and expectation of God. They ran a Sunday School for adults, a Christian elementary school, a Bible school and an evangelism program. We spent all year there

50

and I hardly went anywhere else. It wasn't necessary. It was good to get our roots down in one church and not to chase around to others. Victory Christian Center offered so many things to do and be a part of that it was fully sufficient. We'd never seen a church like it; there was nothing like it at home in Scandinavia. How good it was to be there.

Third, we were in a prayer group that was very dynamic for its time. We prayed for hours, learning to be sensitive in the spirit and to pray several ways in tongues and intercession. The prayer group meant much to us during our year there.

Fourth, it was a spiritually enriching education to see and follow the different ministries. There were many ministers operating under a powerful anointing. Several others from Sweden were there also.

The year at Bible school passed quickly and it was soon time to return to Sweden. One thing I knew: we would start a Bible school in Uppsala. As early as when I was a chaplain to the students I saw the need for a Bible school that taught subjects like Faith, Righteousness, The Covenants, Healing, Praise & Worship and How to be led by the Spirit. Now, I had been to Bible school where I had not only received teaching but I'd also witnessed how one can teach a lot of students at the same time.

One morning, as I was shaving, the Holy Ghost said to me, "Pastor Bror Spetz in Södermalm Church (Stockholm) will call you soon." I'd never met him or been to his church. The only thing I'd ever seen was an advertisement from his church. When I came home from Bible school my wife told me, "A pastor by the name of 'Bror Spetz' phoned for you." I was amazed! He phoned again and invited me to speak at his prayer conference, summer 1982. So I accepted and told him that the Lord had already spoken to me about him. Now it was Bror's turn to be surprised. He was silent for a moment and then confirmed the date.

The closer the time came to our return home to Sweden, the more I thought about what I would do once we arrived. I wanted to travel and teach on faith, but I had no invitations. I had very few contacts in the evangelical churches and the Swedish state church didn't have itinerant preachers. However, I wrote a list of possible places and people I could visit. It numbered sixteen. Looking at that list later, I noted that only one of them had ever called me, but writing the list had helped me feel a little calmer anyway.

Back in Sweden again, a new life was about to begin for us. Just before my trip to the U.S. in 1981, my father-in-law and I had invited two preachers from Tulsa to minister at a very powerful pastors' conference just outside Uppsala. In 1982 it was time again. More preachers came and we sensed that something significant had now been set in motion. After this pastors' conference it was time for the prayer conference at Södermalm Church and following that, invitations to preach were the least of my problems. The Monday morning after the conference at Södermalm, the Lord spoke to me about two things: I was to travel from place to place in Sweden, teaching, and I was also to teach regularly at Södermalm Church. Bror Spetz phoned shortly afterwards, and it happened again; he wondered if I would teach regularly at his Wednesday night meetings. When I told him that the Lord had already talked to me about it, he was quiet for a moment and then we laughed together (Bror and I have always laughed a lot when we've met) and the matter was decided.

An intense year followed. In August our fourth son, Benjamin, was born but I was away for most of his first year. My schedule was full and traveling took up most of my time. But before this, something notable happened. A minister friend who'd attended our first pastors' conference in 1981, asked me if I would accompany him to Bangladesh, that's right—Bangladesh! Money for the ticket was simply not available, so the Lord spoke to a brother who, not knowing why, made a journey of over sixty miles to give me the sizeable sum required to secure it. Once in Bangladesh, the Lord reminded me of the prophecy I had received but not understood. It wasn't wrong. It was just as the prophet had said, but at another time and through another channel.

Those Wednesdays at Södermalm were both glorious and significant. The church was nearly always full and the "word of faith" spread, not only in Stockholm but throughout the land. Without those two years of Wednesday nights, the teaching of faith would not have spread so rapidly or so effectively. Bror Spetz was a key figure used by the Lord for this task and it was a great pleasure to get to know him. Our fellowship has deepened through the years. Bror is a real intercessor with a strong prophetic vein. Our friendship has always been important to me and will remain so.

My father-in-law's network of pastors and friends has also played a significant role. Throughout the years, many of them had received sound teaching on faith from Sten and many were hungry for more. The need for revival and change in Sweden had grown enormous over the years. Hunger for the Word of God and a thirst for the miracle-working gospel was great in the land. The charismatic movement had subsided by this time and the flame was burning low, but only for a time. Faith in the Bible as the Word of God was on the retreat both in theory and in practice—but simmering beneath the surface was a yearning expectation for some new initiative.

CHAPTER FOUR

Word of Life Launched

Throughout the entire year in Tulsa I warded off the thought of starting a new church. I didn't want to. It wasn't the thing you did in Sweden. I didn't know how to go about it and I didn't want to be a pastor. I wanted to be a Bible teacher and an evangelist. The denominations would only try to stop us, I argued.

However, after preaching for a year all over Sweden, teaching regularly at Södermalm church in Stockholm and holding Thursday night meetings in various places in Uppsala, I at last acknowledged the growing need, not only of a Bible school, but also of a church. In those days it was thoroughly controversial to even think of starting a church. There was a kind of unspoken "eleventh commandment" hanging in the air which said: "Thou shalt not start a new church." Such an act would be considered as almost worse than adultery. Behind it, of course, lay fear, prejudice and an ambition for monopoly and control.

Anyhow, Word of Life church was founded on May 24, 1983. In September, Word of Life Bible Center opened. During the summer we had held another pastors' conference, this time at the seashore. It was dynamic. After that, the conferences moved to Uppsala and were called "faith conferences." Later the name was changed to the "Europe Conference."

The church, the Bible school and everything else was founded on one vision:

Equip my people with My word of faith
Show them their spiritual weapons
Teach them how to use them, and
Send them out into victorious battle for the Lord!

About 200 students enrolled the first year—an unprecedented number in Sweden. While the few schools in existence were having great difficulty recruiting people, our students came from all across the land. God drew them to Uppsala. Some scarcely knew why they were coming, but they came anyway. The days were busy; acquiring facilities, teachers, course literature, developing schedules and other things. In September 1983 when the Bible school was officially launched, something new was under way in the country.

None of us who were involved had really much of a clue as to what a far reaching effect this Bible school would have—and it was just as well. Looking back, we can see how God's Word has been spread in Sweden, Scandinavia, Russia and Eastern Europe, and many churches and Bible schools have been established. None of these would exist today had we not responded to the urgency in what the Lord was telling us to do.

It was wonderful to teach the Word of God, and the teachers laboured faithfully, led by His Spirit. This led to a radical change in many people's lives and a new generation of believers began to emerge. The cry for teaching began to be heard from every direction. Soon teaching tapes were being mass-produced and spread everywhere and books were being translated and printed for the Bible school and for the multitudes of hungry people. People began traveling great distances to attend seminars and to receive teaching and prayer.

The church was small at first but it grew steadily. We soon outgrew our rented facilities and had to hold two Sunday meetings in order to serve everyone. Signs and wonders also began to take place in Uppsala and more services were held around the country. Of course, miracles had happened before, but this was something new. Expectations now began to rise on a major scale as the faith of believers began to be revived and people started to believe again that God really did want to heal them and that they really could live in victory.

The expression "to live in victory" was heard increasingly. I began to meet Christians who claimed a little assertively, "We teach this too, you know," or, "This is nothing new," or "We've been saying these things all the time." Now that is both true and false at the same time. Of course all Christians have had the Word of God and of course believers have prayed for the sick, spoken in tongues and believed in victory before, but the fact is that much of this was not at all emphasized. The gospel had become psychologized, traditionalized, cultured—and tamed! The correct words and terminology were still in use, but God also wants to establish His presence, His glory and His power and affirm His gospel with signs and wonders.

For many, faith had been reduced to resigned mental assent, a critical contribution in the public discussions or a mere solution for those in need of counselling-therapy. Actually, faith is a joyful expectation and robust confidence in God that He really can, and will, supernaturally and miraculously answer their prayers. Yet perhaps the most insidious of all was the fact that people, having inherited the correct terminology and procedures and assuming that they had a monopoly on the truth, thought they had it all. But the kingdom of God is not in word but in power (1 Cor 4:20).

The expression, "to live in victory" doesn't mean a life free of problems, of course. The Bible doesn't promise a life of comfort and self-gratification; it speaks of trials, tests and attacks. But *"in all these things we are more than conquerors through him who loved us."* (Rom 8:37). Knowing the truth of this word kept us on course during the turbulence surrounding the start of the Bible school... and that which continued during the next 5 years.

We could not have predicted the intense, compact resistance that came from Christians and non-Christians alike. After an editorial (warning and cautioning people about Word of Life) appeared in "the Messenger," a Swedish Evangelical Mission Newspaper, it was picked up and printed in the Pentecostal national daily, "The Day." The secular press then began to launch its attacks. Actually, the persecution was all rather strange and unnecessary, but the spiritual climate was so tense in the country that the abuse came as a kind of release valve for the pressure. Persecution increased in intensity until the onslaught in the morning and evening papers lost all sense of proportion and objectivity and finally became hysterical.

Firstly, within the Christian faith there has always been room for differing persuasions, but this attack was then followed by a stigmatization of Word of Life and branding it as a sect, along with charges of "heresy" and "brain-washing." Major contributing causes were relentless coverage in press, radio and TV. During those first years, 1983-1988, the pressure was enormous, more intense, I believe, than most people (who weren't there) can imagine.

Our ministry was launched in the form of a legal trust and this was like waving a red flag in front of a bull. From the press, cries for public scrutiny were heard. Other people questioned the democracy in the church and still more wondered where the elders were to be found. Some got worked up about the church's name and others about the fact that we had ushers. Some people got upset about the size and height of the platform and others about the plexiglas podium. Some complained about the volume of the music, or the clapping, or the dancing or the uplifted hands.

At one time, there seemed to be no end to what "suddenly-religious" Sweden thought was wrong with us. The remarkable thing was that no one asked if the Lord was present or if his power was seen among us. Looking back, one can see what a tough job of ploughing it really was. A plough is used for ploughing, and we'd received a prophetic word that the church was like a plough. So we just kept on ploughing!

In it all, God's word bore fruit. For every complaint, criticism or attack there was a superabundance of happy reports of transformed lives. Everything seemed to be happening. People were being saved and miraculously healed, others had their breakthroughs or were baptized in the Spirit. And it was all worth it! More people joined the church and more applications rolled in for the Bible school. Something was clearly on the move.

Obviously our church was different. Everything, from the name and the structure and the legal trust, to the order of the services, all was very different. And of course it did feel unfamiliar and unconventional to some Christians. But to take the next step and say it was wrong was rather steep. For one thing, the Bible doesn't say which legal entity a church should be. There is an obvious freedom. The fact that Word of Life is a legal trust doesn't make it any less a church.

A church must be defined according to biblical, not legal, principles. Of course it must be open to public scrutiny to ensure that it is run lawfully and that its finances are in order. This is its point of interaction with the world. But if this is the case, and auditors and government inspectors etc are satisfied, then operations are clearly legally correct.

Word of Life has been a trust from the start and although operations have greatly expanded and altered, the authorities have had no complaints. We have engaged a well-known firm of accountants, who are neither Christian nor linked with us in any way, and one by one our "accusers" have fallen silent.

Biblically, Word of Life must demonstrate New Testament life, doctrine and power. Controversial issues like, "elders", are irrelevant. To think, for example, that using the term "elder", makes a church Biblical and alive is self-deception. Though we do not use that title, this function is possibly performed more effectively than in some other churches that do use the title. The Biblical evidence of our church is found more in brotherly love, heart-unity in the lives of the individual believers and evangelism efforts etc. I am not trying to counter anyone here. I am writing to illustrate the humor—or tragedy—of these discussions while we should have all shown more love and faith and the anointing and manifestation of the Spirit. Just as the Swedish Church once had to tolerate the emergence of evangelical churches and admit that God was using them, so must these, in turn, also endorse God's work in other forms and expressions.

Our church has grown both numerically and spiritually. We are often asked if we've changed. We must appear to have, for some have begun to accept us. The answer is both yes and no. No, because the basis of our vision, theology, work and views remains the same. In these, there is really no change. But then one must remember; our views have so little in common with the mass-media's (Christian or secular) sometimes ghastly descriptions of us.

The answer to the question as to whether we've changed can also be, "yes". Naturally, we've changed. Everything changes, and that includes us. We have gained experience, received more insight, made mistakes and matured and so on. We are not the same today as when we started. No one can be. But, several things have remained constant and unchanging through the years. We have the same

Bible, the same gospel, the same Jesus and the same Holy Spirit!

An operation of the size that we are today, touching thousands of lives, is obviously different from a church of a 100 as we were in our first year. I sometimes think our members themselves can be tempted to forget it. We can indeed remember some specially powerful meetings, but today we're reaching 100 times more people in many more fields. That represents growth such as God promised us from the beginning, and we've seen it come by degrees.

Growth can be measured in many ways. Statistics is one. It doesn't tell you everything, but it tells you some things. In the Acts of the Apostles, Luke, the evangelist, quotes certain figures when recounting church growth. We use statistics, not to outdo or outshine others, but because church growth is a natural part of Christian life. Jesus himself said, *"This is to my Father's glory, that you bear much fruit, showing yourselves to be my disciples"* (John 15:8).

That is why it is important and joyful to notice there is a growth and increase in the church and all of its aspects year by year.

But all growth entails new challenges. We needed more qualified leaders, more staff and consequently, more money. Many of our workers were inexperienced or newly saved young Christians. Even if the anointing is powerful in meetings, there are practical sides to church work that must be considered. We all make mistakes, especially in the beginning. Maturity and sanctification is needed how ever strong the anointing might be in meetings... and it really was. Sometimes, people lay prostrate under the power of God; sometimes the spirit of intercession came upon

us and we prayed for hours. At other times a powerful prophetic anointing came upon us. At those times
the Lord encouraged or admonished us and pointed
the way ahead.

While all this was going on, sensation-hungry journalists and sceptical theologians from religious
denominations came and sat in our meetings. No
wonder we were publicized, criticized and scandal-
ized. Reports of earlier revivals and similar happen-
ings made encouraging reading! Then, as now, out of
the general "hullabaloo" and obvious flaws, something powerful still emerged—with God's help. This
has often been a strengthening comfort to me when
the cannons have thundered on every side.

In those early years, it was remarkable how the
teaching of faith began to grip people's hearts. But
what is "faith teaching"? It can be simply stated:
knowing from God's word, the Bible, 1) who God is,
what he has and what he can, and will, do, 2) who the
believer is, what he has and what he can do in Christ
Jesus, and 3) who the enemy is, what he has (and
doesn't have) and can do (and can't do). In other
words it is the fundamental Bible teaching concerning the position and power of the believer and his life
in Christ Jesus.

To understand this we have to see what God's
word says about who God is. We must know His
character, His kindness (James 1:17; 1 John 4:8) and
His covenant with man. We have to understand what
happened on the cross and how God's righteousness
was made ours in Christ (2 Cor. 5:21). We need to see
that when Jesus was made a curse on the cross, it
opened the way for the blessing of Abraham to
become ours (Gal. 3;13-14). We will then understand

our legal position as believers in Christ Jesus, how the covenant blessings, protection and life are ours by grace (Rom. 5:12) and how we, by faith, (the gift of God), receive his blessings and live in them.

This enables us to see in the Word of God how the believer has faith, how it comes, how it works, how it is activated, how it overcomes and how it receives from God (Rom. 10:17; Philem. v. 6; Heb 11:1, 6; 1 John 5:4-5). We see how faith is the faith of the heart (Rom. 10:9) which is directly linked with the confession of the mouth (Mark 11:23; Rom. 10:9) and how faith without works is dead (James 2:26). In God's covenant, we have been blessed with all the spiritual blessings in the heavenly places in Christ Jesus (Eph. 1:3). Our heart-faith which comes from the promises of God receives these blessings in every area of or lives (3 John v. 2).

As God's word enters the believer, the enemy has to retreat from area after area of his life (James 4:7; 1 Pet. 5:8). His personal victory in Christ Jesus is established (Eph. 6:10-13) and the Spirit of God does miracles, pours in his superabundant life and leads him on, step by step further into God's plan.

He overcomes the devil's opposition, clearly described in the Bible, using the authority given him in Jesus' name (Luke 10:19; John 16:24) and his spiritual weapons: the sword of the Spirit which is the Word of God (Eph. 6:13-17), the blood of Jesus (Rev. 12:11), Jesus' name (Phil. 2:9-10), the Spiritual gifts (1 Cor. 12), prayer (Mark 11:23-24), fasting (Mark 9:29) and the word of his testimony (Rev. 12:11). Each of these things overcomes the blockades thrown up by the enemy, and believers who have suffered defeat, been disarmed, weighed down and confused can find freedom, victory and a whole new boldness!

Our stand, concerning victory and liberty, are the grounds upon which the theological war has basically been fought. Really, it has been an attack on our courage, because we've dared to be bold enough to proclaim the liberty and victory of every Christian, to proclaim the Christian's position of righteousness before God in Christ Jesus as legal ground for receiving answers to prayers, and seeing miracles take place and experiencing victory. The battle has been over the Christian's liberty or captivity.

Now no-one insists that a Christian can be sinlessly perfect or enjoy total success and never have any problems in life. That's a travesty of true faith teaching. On the contrary, there can be even more problems. The Bible speaks in clear terms about the spiritual battle for the lives of men and women and how the flesh wars against the spirit (1 Pet. 2:11), but it also speaks about the possibilities now open through faith in Jesus (Mark 9:23, 1:23-24; John 14:12; 1 John 5:4-5).

In an environment where spiritual gifts and signs and wonders were scarce, where prophecy and revelation were scorned, where doubt and unbelief lay like a smothering blanket upon the Word of God and where God wasn't expected to do anything, faith teaching was a necessity. No matter how fierce the opposition against it, no matter what the objections may be, we can never get away from the fact that Romans 1:17 says, *"In the gospel a righteousness from God is revealed, a righteousness that is by faith from first to last, as it is written: 'The righteous will live by faith'."*

It is through the grace of God that we are saved. It is by that grace we stand, and never by our own works. But grace is received by faith (Eph. 2:8-9; John 1:12) and this superabundant life is lived out by faith. That is why Paul is so pleased with the church in Thessalonica, when he sees that their faith *"...is growing more and more"* (2 Thess. 1:3). That, too, is why Jesus says about faith, *"Assuredly, I say to you, if you have faith and do not doubt, you will not only do what was done to the fig tree, but also if you say to this mountain, 'Be removed and be cast into the sea,' it will be done. And whatever things you ask in prayer, believing, you will receive."* (Matt. 21:21-22).

It is the job of every preacher to encourage and inspire people to let faith take root in their hearts and actively seek God on the ground of His promises, while expecting every good thing from Him. Should this be done, every church would become a "faith church," i. e. a church consisting of people who love and believe God, reverence His word, stand on His promises, expect wonders and miracles, while living in God's supernatural realm, abounding in the life of the Spirit, proclaiming the full gospel and expecting Jesus to return.

I am convinced that God is raising up an army of victorious, conquering Christians from every background and persuasion, wherever He can find believers. He isn't raising up a group of Christians who are invincible conquerers in themselves. They aren't a super-elite group of Christians. They are ordinary people in fellowship with the living God. They are not perfect people, but people with the Perfect One, Jesus Christ, inside them. They're believers in covenant with God who know that all the covenant blessings belong to them. They are believers who, though weak in themselves, derive their power from God's grace (2 Tim. 2:1) and are strong *"in the Lord and in His mighty power"* (Eph. 6:10).

Faith teaching can be summed up simply as God's way of liberating the believer, so that he can live in victory. Then he can really obey God and go out, win the lost and complete the Great Commission. If there is anything the enemy of souls doesn't want, it is that we should win the lost for God. Therefore, it is not difficult to understand why the enemy poses opposition to faith teaching.

We should not think it strange that there was a commotion. When Christians look into the Word of God, see who they are, what they have and what they can do, they become bold and active—and the community reacts. A secularized society can tolerate passive Christians who don't go out, don't rise up and influence or actively evangelize the community and who do not expect God to endorse His word with open miracles. But when believers become active, mobilize, begin praying earnestly for revival and go out with the gospel, they immediately meet with strife, scorn and scandal. That is the price believers have paid in every generation, and it is worth it if the gospel impacts the nation and the land turns to God.

Despite the opposition it was tremendously encouraging to see God work and hear about people's lives being transformed. With the formation of Word of Life, an invisible barrier was broken through and the field was open for establishing new churches. New churches sprang up across Sweden. Many of them, (not all), were inspired by God. In some cases, they were birthed by His Spirit; in others, it was through human effort and will-power.

It is not impossible or contrary to God's will to start a new church. Nor is there any intrinsic value in starting something new. The important thing was that a precedent had been set. What was from God would stand, what was from man would fall.

CHAPTER FIVE

Accusations and Persecutions

I t soon became apparent that the teaching of faith caused a reaction that was like a spiritual bomb exploding with a devastating effect. I could never have foreseen that the blast would be so powerful. Word of Life church soon became the main media serial-story for weeks on end.

Obviously, there were many reasons for it. The concern that spread through the evangelical churches, though partly legitimate, was, however, generally exaggerated. Questions asked such as: "What is all of this about?", "Is it heresy?", "Is it a sect?", were for the most part justified. The problem lay in the fact that it was often deeply critical people or worse—the evening papers—that were permitted to supply the answers, so that reasonable concern became a deep-seated prejudice.

The man in the street wondered. His usual source of information, the mass media, depicted that something horrendous had struck Sweden. Eventually, a TV program host summed it up this way. He asked one of our decriers sarcastically if Word of Life had not indeed become Sweden's "spittoon", and should we not be "outlawed"? Furthermore should it not be concluded that every thing we do is automatically wrong; and if this is so, would it not be "politically correct" (in todays terms) to say everyone should spit at us?

In a land such as Sweden, with secularization escalating and de-christianization at epidemic proportions, we can see clearly, Word of Life was like a spiritual shock treatment. To quote pastor Sven Nilsson, "Word of Life was necessary." This is not to justify everything we did, but to establish that God earnestly wanted to awake His church, arrest Sweden's attention and effectively spread the gospel throughout the nation.

Opposition now began to mount on several fronts. Christians from the liberal school, aided by psychologists, journalists and theologians, launched the attack. Those denominational Christians who felt accused or insulted or felt their monopoly threatened took their stand. The secular press, ignorant of the rudiments of Christian truth, joined the confused fight. Politicians who felt reproached reacted. A few people who left Word of Life were called "escapees" by the press; they too added their voice.

Coming, as it did, from so many angles, this crossfire only compounded the problem. Trying to answer journalists, some of whom lacked the most elementary knowledge of the Bible, Christianity or theology, or replying to an upset Pentecostal who said we were on the wrong track, was not an easy task. In addition, an answer to a single question was interpreted differently by each group present and then sometimes twisted beyond recognition.

The same thing happened when I was qouted. On occasions my words were taken completely out of context from a sermon or from a tape. For example, a journalist could take my laughter from a tape and play it repeatedly on TV or radio until it sounded bizarre. Another favorite trick was to cut a sentence from an exhortation before the offering was taken up and repeat it over and over. Of course every evangelist and evangelical preacher knows that he sometimes raises his voice and shouts. The secularized journalists couldn't make the association with old-time revival preachers or, even Jesus himself: *"On the last and greatest day of the feast, Jesus stood and said in a loud voice..."* (John 7:37). Their associations went to Hitler. None of them seemed to notice that though many people came to the meetings they still didn't shout as loud as they do at sporting events. Big meetings, crowds, a high platform and a preacher who shouted—the journalists' conclusions were simple—I was a new Hitler.

Sometimes the reporters actions were totally ignorant, malicious and prejudiced. On occasions they would say, "But you said it!" Sure, it was on tape but it had been taken totally out of context. But because "I had said it", the field was open for everyone to misquote me. Of course, not everything I said was the "Word of God" or completely right. In the heat of battle some statements I made were unnecessarily sharp and to the point.

We have never believed that everything a preacher says is always, automatically from God. Everything a preacher says must be examined in the light of Scripture, the highest norm. It is the right and duty of every believer to *"examine the Scriptures to see if what is said is true"*. (Acts. 17:11). But if a scripture-scorning reporter gets worked up because a preacher believes in a heaven and a hell, it is certain his report will not be favorable. And it doesn't help matters to know that the papers in Sweden are not keen on correcting articles or printing replies, to put it mildly!

Harassment increased, reaching a peak on a TV show called "20:00." In all of Swedish TV history it will be hard to find anything as twisted and perverted as the harrassment we received. Surley we had been too naive believing that if TV were to send a program about us, they would treat us objectively. How could we have known that their agenda was already fixed? We didn't know that Tom Alandh, the editor, would cut out all the positive interviews, place his cameras on the floor to film distorted angles and then add negative comments to the otherwise positive shots?

The reaction of the people in the country was furious and unrelenting. There was outrageously strong protests against us, and a rerun of the program brougth another onslaught.. Strangely, reporters and some religious debaters wondered why we became more restrictive to these kinds of interviews. They accused us of being unwilling to talk which confirmed to them the accuracy of their criticism.

What a farce it was. What hatred arose. But I well remember a phone call right after the scandalous program. Somebody in a convalescent home had watched the program with a friend. When the sequence of speaking in tongues was rerun, both were convicted of sin, climbed in a car, drove to Word of Life and were saved! Similar things happened all the time, and we were greatly encouraged by the Lord.

I believe that members who've joined us since then would benefit from knowing more about those early days. Every thing we enjoy today came with a sacrifice. Every change and breakthrough had its price. We knew there was only one way—forward, and the outcome—victory. The Lord comforted us time and again with words like those in Matt. 5:10-12: *"Blessed are those who are persecuted because of righteousness, for theirs is the kingdom of heaven. Blessed are you when people insult you, persecute you and falsely say all kinds of evil against you because of me. Rejoice and be glad, because great is your reward in heaven, for in the same way they persecuted the prophets who were before you."*

Such great love and encouragement came from many Christians. Letters flooded in and people sent flowers and Bible verses. It was tremendous to see the reactions of Christians from different backgrounds. The greater the antagonism, the more the Lord helped us, and the stronger we became and the more our numbers increased.

These onslaughts have come in waves, and the remarkable thing is, the church has become more and more united under the pressure. Though the press made a great fuss of those who left us, in reality, it was only a few.

All of the talk about the "escapees" was exaggerated and ridiculous. They were pictured in the newspapers making the most fantastic statements. On further investigation, however, it was found that the brief rush of articles were quoting the same few people, sometimes under fictitious names. For a time, some of them were allowed to elaborate and say anything at all and the press swallowed it all. Some of these "escapees" stood for a completely worldly lifestyle, one was a homosexual and others were simply dissatisfied with us. The State Church took some to its bosom, but some of them made themselves impossible there, also.

Personally, I don't find these "escapees" any great problem. The problem was more a moral issue—how the de-christianized press could use them to the degree they did, and how they could distort truth when that truth didn't suit their opinions.

Now I am not blaming everything on the so called "escapees" or the press. Of course we made our mistakes. What we must look at, above all, is the intention. Was our intention to harm people, bind them up or take their money from them? Of course not. Was our intention to create a sect-like party cut off from society. Never! But that was how it was depicted.

The question is really more central. Is there room in Sweden today to practice the gospel, to believe the Bible and expect God to do miracles today? Yes, I am convinced that there is room in Sweden today for the gospel, the full gospel!

But there is a battle for this territory. The remarkable thing is that while the media has fought us they have introduced one occult phenomenon after another. New Age prophetesses, witches, shamans, astral-walkers and their related sort are seen regularly on the screen. It appears that this kind of supernatural phenomenon is accepted on entirely different basis than the supernatural gospel. These bizarre, occult phenomena never lead to conversion and salvation. Only the gospel does that. People like the supernatural that doesn't call for repentence and a holy life towards God. The occult suits them fine.

The gospel without God's power is unfruitful and pitiful. In Acts 8:5-8 Philip came to Samaria and preached Christ there: *"When the crowds heard Philip and saw the miraculous signs he did, they all paid close attention to what he said. With shrieks, evil spirits came out of many, and many paralytics and cripples were healed. So there was great joy in that city."*

Philip preached Christ in the power of the Spirit. People were saved, healed and freed from evil spirits. Here, we come to a sensitive subject: healing and deliverance. First, it is important to see that the gospels, and, the whole New Testament, speak plainly of these things. It isn't a sectarian doctrine, but fundamental, New Testament Christianity.

Second, it is deplorable that certain parts of the church in Sweden have fallen flat in the face of secularized rationalism. In their eagerness to please men, and the modern, somewhat supercilious, secularized Swedish society, they have taken away vital parts of the gospel and are embarrassed about Jesus as the gospels describe Him.

It was when we began praying for the sick and seeing people healed that shameful lies began to circulate about us. Among the worst was the charge that we despised the disabled and treated them disgracefully. Nothing I answered or wrote helped. This prejudice stuck and naturally aroused anger.

It would be too much to take up individual cases, though it would be interesting to see the different picture that would emerge. Nor can I or the staff endorse everything any overzealous Bible school student might have said or done (we have graduated over 6 000 to date) but we know, for certain the truth of what we have taught.

First, everybody has the same, unique value irrespective of background, talent, ability, race or gender. God who has created all loves all equally.

Secondly, we have never taught that a person is a greater sinner because he is sick. Absurd charge! Nor have we taught that sickness is a punishment from God.

To find that being taught, one must go to old Lutheran or Roman Catholic doctrine. What we have said is that sin, sickness, poverty, hate, war, anxiety, loneliness and death entered the world through the fall. This is basic Bible teaching. This means that the origin of sin, sickness, selfishness and death is not God but the enemy of souls. The Bible confirms this plainly in Gen 3:1-19; Luke 13:16; John 10:10; Acts 10:38 and Rom. 5:12-19.

The solution to every problem of man lies in Jesus' death on the cross. The Son of God did not come to take, but to give. According to Scripture (Isa. 53:3-5, 10-11; Matt. 8:16-17; 1 Pet. 2:24), Jesus carried away our sins, our sicknesses, our anxiety and death and *"by His wounds we are healed"* (Isa. 53:5). Jesus showed this as He *"went about doing good and healing all who were under the power of the devil, because God was with him"* (Acts 10:38).

In other words, there is an offer of healing in the gospel due to Jesus' death by crucifixion and by His example as He healed the sick. We neither criticize, belittle nor condemn the sick. We have been falsely accused of despising the weak and I think nothing has stung me more. It's wrong, it's shameful and it's cowardly!

These charges cannot stand in the light of what we preach and practice, yet some journalists still revel in accusing us of them today. What is more, we have disabled people in our church: the deaf, those in wheelchairs and many others who are happy among us because of the help they receive and the care and understanding their families have received in the positive environment of our church. If I were sick, I'd rather be in an environment where people pray and encourage me than where they deny me hope or the possibility of being healed or say, that it is God who put the sickness on me to teach me something for some unknown reason.

A few words about deliverance from evil spirits. The Bible speaks about it. Christians have commonly avoided it and the world doesn't understand it. But Jesus delivered people all the time. Naturally there is going to be a commotion about this kind of issue and of course, things can get out of balance. There are two ditches: under-emphasis to sheer denial on the one hand and over-emphasis on the other. I will not give a Biblical discourse here on "evil spirits," but something must be said.

To teach about the existence of the devil and evil spirits and their activities and influence is on no account unbiblical. Conversely, with so much occult activity, eastern religion, alcohol, drugs and abnormal sexual activity all around, sound teaching is even more necessary. On this point some have accused us of exalting the devil and diminishing Jesus. Never! Jesus is Lord! Jesus is our Redeemer! Jesus is our Saviour and Shepherd! But the Bible tells us that He has disarmed the devil and put him to shame (Luke 11:14-23; Col. 2:15; Heb. 2:14-15). If secularized journalists don't understand it, that is one thing, but believers should be more faithful to the abiding Word of God than to views that are "here today and gone tomorrow."

Many Bible teachers visited us for seminars at the Bible school. Some of them were a great help at the outset, specially when teaching on prayer and righteousness, but after some time they laid the emphasis increasingly on deliverance from evil spirits. At the start, this wasn't extraordinary. Several teachers, for example, Lester Sumrall, visiting us for the first time in 1985, shared his vast experience of deliverances from the mission field around the world. Other staff, besides myself, had witnessed people being radically delivered in different Christian circles both in and out of the country.

But these ministers increasingly radicalized the doctrine. Strange reports of their methods reached us. Finally, the pastors and I called them in to take up some clearly non-biblical tendencies. They got very upset and didn't take kindly to our questioning. I made the decision not to invite them to speak anymore and they were dismayed. However, I couldn't throw out everything the Bible has to say about deliverance. Lester Sumrall was a great help here. We didn't want a split in the church because of the teaching, so I took things slowly. Looking back, I see I should have acted more swiftly.

The accusations were many and the billows rolled. All the time, the church grew. God was inconceivably good towards us even when we made mistakes and were found wanting. It seemed that His blessings found a way through the barrages of everything leveled against us. The pressure was sometimes extreme. Besides hate-filled letters and looks that could kill, the pressure was so intense at times that one could hardly breathe. I forced myself to go downtown like a normal person, though it wasn't a relaxation, to put it mildly. Sometimes my head was whirling with insistent thoughts: Give up! Run! Get out! So I just had to endure and plough on.

Without the prayers of hundreds, indeed, thousands of people, I would never have made it. To go downtown and feel the compact hatred was a horrendous experience. Seeing a cashier turn her head away while she gave me the change wasn't nice, just as hearing voices howling curses at us in the street outside our home in the evening wasn't either. Getting our fence pulled up, beer bottles and condoms thrown into the garden and pornographic mail sent to my wife, our walls sprayed with paint and stones through our windows was a major trial. We even got our car tires slashed and the paintwork stripped. Seeing my name in the news flyers wasn't easy for our kids either.

I remember a trip to Finland on the plane. Every other person was reading the same evening paper, all open at the same page and all staring at a huge picture of me and reading the adjoining hate-article. No wonder the person beside me looked a little suspiciously at me sitting quietly reading the Bible.

It was a wonderful experience to see God protect the children. In the midst of it all the sun smiled down on them, though they got their share of the paddle. It was worst for my son Aron who was at high school and heard both one and two things. Seeing the flyers with his dad portrayed as a "crazy sect-leader" wasn't easy. It hit him hard on occasions, but the hardest to bear was the extremely deriding attitude of other Christians.

Little Benjamin came home distressed one day saying that a big boy had threatened to hammer a big nail through his brains. Jonatan was sitting reading Asterix in his room and came to a picture of a balloon with the words "Crash, bang!" Just then, "Crash!", a stone smashed through his window and landed on the floor.

On occasions it was both tragic and comical. One day, reporters from both of the main evening papers showed up on the doorstep simultaneously while the debate about our teaching on spanking was in full swing. Just then the little boys started playing with sticks, big Samuel said to Benjamin while swinging a stick, "Now you just need a little taste of this!" Of all moments to joke about it, they chose that one!

It wasn't much fun for Jonatan, when going to school one day, on a wall he saw two foot high letters spelling out "HANG ULF EKMAN!" But the climax was the two bomb attacks. One exploded in the foyer at Word of Life and destroyed it. About the same time, Uppsala had been smeared in more than 100 places with a devilish logo and the words "Dödens Ord" (The word of death). The other bomb blew up at our home one night at 9 p.m. It had been deposited in our armour-plated mail box (our boxes had been smashed regularly and our mail destroyed or stolen). The mail box and parts of the fence were blown to a thousand pieces and shrapnel was scattered every-where. The police were visibly shaken when they saw that the person placing the bomb had used dynamite. Had anyone been passing, they would have been killed.

Looking back, the hatred seems unreal, but it was almost tangible at the time. The police came to our home and asked if I wanted a personal police guard, but I declined. On the other hand, we intensified the watch around Word of Life, and it was necessary, we found out later. A satanist was found sitting in his car in the parking lot armed with a hand grenade. In a meeting in another town, satan-worshippers came armed to shoot me, but no shots were ever fired.

Today I meet Christians from some circles who like to play things down by saying, "It wasn't really so bad during the 80s was it." Well, I don't know where they were, but for us, the antagonism was extremly real! And yet so blessed! Time and again we were forced to the Lord in prayer and had to rely on Him for continuing miracles. It was in the midst of all this that He told us to start our new building! God really proved that He is independent of man's opinion to do want He wants to do.

CHAPTER SIX

The new Building

The services were full to overflowing. We were outgrowing our premises on Axel Johansson Street. The name of the street is interesting. Axel Johansson, legendary chief editor of The Uppsala News, was a renowned opposer of Christianity. It was God's sense of humor to put us on his street—and we're still there today. We began praying for a place to build and searched all over Uppsala for the right location.

Turning onto Axel Johansson St. on my way to the Bible school one morning, I glanced at the site opposite the building we were renting. It was empty! I'd never thought about it before. It was as though I saw it for the first time, and it "glowed." It was an awesome experience. I phoned the local authorities about the property, and a surprised officer replied, "It's remarkable that you called now, we're just about to divide that site." It was by the grace of God that we weren't too late.

In our early, planning phase, we met an architect, Lars Hallgren, from Gothenburg. Lars became a vital help to us in many ways, and a warm friendship arose. At first, we envisioned a building to seat 1 000-1 500 but the more we planned the more the Lord increased our faith until we arrived at 4 000. It was a gigantic project for a church of 200-300 members.

We were given a six-month option on the site, which means, we had first privileges to buy. Six months later we requested an extension and got it. After another half-year we asked for another six months extension and got it, though the local authorities began to raise their eyebrows. This was our last extension. To keep the site, we were forced to buy it, but we hardly had any money. All this time the customary attacks and witch-hunt raged on and at such times people are not inclined to give. We were constantly accused by the media of misusing money, swindling the people and that the offerings went straight into my pocket.

But the money kept rolling in! There was, and is, an enormous generosity among our members, Bible school students and visitors. It was unthinkable that such a little church could manage such a large building project, but God provided us with intercessors and donors across the land. The day came when we must purchase the lot, and the money to the last coin was in the account. Afterwards we were penniless—but we had a building site.

Before the purchase we had talked with planning consultants. They weren't used to anyone coming to them with plans, while having no building site. Finally, one lost patience and burst out, "Do you have a building site or don't you?" I replied, "Of course we have a site." What I meant was "Yes, we have one by faith. We haven't bought it yet but we will when we get a little more money." He wasn't much the wiser.

In the end we secured the lot—but had nothing left to build with. That was in January 1986. Our goal was to have the building complete by July 1987, which meant we had to start right away. We continued collecting money (we needed 18 million Swedish crowns or 2,5 million U.S. dollars) but the little we had at the time took us nowhere. No building company was crazy enough to start building without bank backing, least of all, for Word of Life.

We contacted banks—a new and different sphere for us, the reply was the same, "Word of Life? Sorry, no loan possible." It was the same story everywhere, sometimes coupled with extreme contempt. In one bank I thought the director was about to spit in my face. There was a blank, complete "No" to all our efforts. Dagens Nyheter, Sweden's leading daily paper learned of our plans and wrote a sarcastic article about it adding that they would probably come to nothing. But we prayed, and prayed and prayed, though we seemed to get nowhere, and soon it would be too late for getting the building ready for the summer conference in 1987.

Patsy Behrman and Mary-Alice Isleib came from Oklahoma to speak at a seminar. In one meeting, Patsy felt we should all leave the premises, and the men should form a broad front and run the length of the site praying aloud. We did it. We ran like maniacs shouting in tongues. What a sight it must have made! A brother said afterwards that he'd seen a vision of massive demonic resistance leaving the site.

After this things began to change. Pastor Spetz introduced us to a bank in Stockholm that wasn't entirely closed to us, and now things looked promising. However, nothing was certain yet. We decided to break the ground without money. The church assembled on the site. We prayed and praised God as we put the spade in the ground. It was a step of faith, but everything we did, we did in faith.

Now faith is the substance of things hoped for, the evidence of things not seen. You know that you know that you know that you have it because of what God has promised, and you hold on firmly and act according to the promise till the answer comes. The Bible also speaks of faith as a spiritual gift (1 Cor. 12:9). In 2 Cor. 4:13 Paul talks about the *"spirit of faith."*

I believe that the gift of faith was placed in my heart for our building. We met such resistance and many difficulties and yet I never felt it hard going. That was supernatural!

We worked hard on the loan. I was due to go on vacation with my family and only the day before had things begun to happen. We were to drive to Gothenburg, take the ferry to Kiel and drive from there to Spain. The day we left, I called from several places to check progress. Only hours before we boarded the ferry did the loan go through. On the boat, as you can guess, I sighed a big sigh of relief!

Once home again, the work began in earnest. First the earthmoving and then hammering of hundreds of poles down into the Uppsala clay. They laid the concrete bed and finally raised the superstructure. It was an interesting time in many ways. I had no experience of building and we joked about our "building committee" consisting of a one-time priest a missionary, who'd put up tin huts in Tanzania, a dealer in gems and a physiotherapist. But Praise God for our architect and consultants!

In meetings with the main contractors we learned a lot. They asked questions about things we knew nothing about, but step by step we pulled through. Money kept coming in all the time from donors throughout the land. I visited the site daily and watched the structure grow. It was a relaxation from Bible school, counselling and church work though it wasn't big at the time.

How exciting it was to build! The building structure rose bit by bit, first the pillars then the beams, after that the roof and walls and finally the rooms and the interior. Thousands of chairs had to be bought. We negotiated the best prices for the best fittings. We had to order carpeting, choose colors and patterns, design the stairs and platform and prepare for a balcony that was to be built two years later with an extra 1.500 seats.

You can imagine the excitement for the church as the construction finally started to take shape, and the vision appeared in reality. Everyone felt that "this is our building." The voluntary contributions and labors were enormous. From the beginning we had taught that the church is a place where willing workers can find their place to help. Not everyone can be employed in a church nor can all the work in a church be done by employees. The Lord has a place and work for every member and the ministry of each believer is both spiritual and practical. Each must do the works of Jesus: testify, pray, be led by the Spirit and serve in practical things.

When the members saw this, it was fantastic to witness the practical help they gave. They helped with night security, child-care, sticking labels on tapes, cleaning the bathrooms and evangelism. There were ushers, offering custodians, intercessors, and building labourers... There was no end to their contributions and to their sacrificial labors of love.

A non-Christian cannot begin to imagine the joy that service brings the believer. That we, in the midst of the church, the Body of Christ, can serve Jesus and one another both "spiritually" and "practically." In the true sense of the Word, all work led by God's Spirit serving both Him and our fellowman, is spiritual.

In some circles, certain Christians have been too high minded and exclusive to get their hands dirty and help practically. They've been too tied up with their own "spiritual" ministry to help practically where it was most needed at the time. That is not how it was with us. People came a long way to help. Their efforts then and now are enormous. This made the entire project clearly supernatural, and I think it should be classed as a "mighty deed."

We received a prophetic word that this building would be a "sign to make people wonder" and that is what has happened. Many have been amazed and speechless, partly by the size of the building, but also by all the daily activities and all the people going out and coming in.

The Opening Day finally arrived. It was by the time of the Faith Conference 1987. We were ready to burst with excitement. The building was packed—more than 5 000 were present, when Lester Sumrall, especially invited for the occasion, held the opening speech. He consecrated the entire building to God and His honor and glory, to Jesus and His gospel and

Great Commission, and to the Holy Spirit, His presence and supernatural life.

That day marked a milestone, not only in the history of Uppsala city, but far exceeding that. We had a definite sense that we were stepping right into the next phase of the vision. The whole week was fantastic. The conference was dynamic, and of course, the press was there. A few weeks earlier the archbishop had promised to collect a million Swedish crowns (130 000 U.S. dollars) to put a stop to Word of Life, but I believe the generosity of those who were with us was greater! On the Wednesday night we took up an offering for the building. It was probably the largest cash collection ever made in Sweden. Including pledges, it totaled 4,5 million Swedish crowns (or 600 000 U.S. dollars), and of course this made news! Not only was money given, but cars, shotguns, jars of honey, jewelery, a cow, Persian mats and much, much more.

We had taken up tithes and offerings from the start, but it seemed that the media had no idea that this was customary in all the evangelical churches since the turn of the century. The news papers wrote and wrote and wrote. Praise God for our professional auditors. Thanks to them no-one could accuse us of irregularities. The Express, an evening paper, alleged there was no check on where the money went, but we weren't in the habit of sending the Express our monthly report. But, our records were available to members, auditors, banks and inspectors.

Wanting to avoid all unclarity, we followed advice and engaged a professional and independent firm of authorized accountants. They've scrutinized everything and we've gained by it. Money is a sensitive subject and rumors spread quickly even among Christians. Perhaps it stirred up "bad blood" in some circles when they saw our collections were large and they heard we taught boldly on the blessings of giving.

The expression, "prosperity teaching" began to be used and we were accused of promising the moon to all who gave to our work. That wasn't so, but we fearlessly preached what God's Word says about it. Here, I believe that people, and especially pastors, have backed down. Some have been too ashamed to take up collections. Others, while quietly bypassing verses that talk about the blessings of giving, have tried crying or threatening the people into giving instead of building them up in faith. But Paul says plainly, *"Whoever sows sparingly will also reap sparingly, and whoever sows generously will also reap generously. Each man should give what he has decided in his heart, not reluctantly or under compulsion, for God loves a cheerful giver. And God is able to make all grace abound to you, so that in all things at all times, having all that you need, you will abound in every good work. As it is written: 'He has scattered abroad his gifts to the poor; his righteousness endures forever.' Now He who supplies seed to the sower, and bread for food, will also supply and increase your store of seed and will enlarge the harvest of your righteousness. You will be made rich in every way so that you can be generous on every occasion, and through us your generosity will result in thanksgiving to God."* (2 Cor. 9:6-11).

It has been frowned upon to say that if you give you'll get. But this is what the Bible plainly teaches. A farmer sows to reap, and Paul calls our money seed in verses 6 and 10. He also says in verse 11 that when we sow we will be enriched in everything. In verse 8 he goes even further saying that God is able to make all grace abound to us so that we'll always have all sufficiency in everything and can give to every good work.

Jesus takes up the same principle in Luke 6:38 when He says, *"Give and it will be given to you, a good measure, pressed down, shaken together and running over will be poured into your lap."* The gospel is free, but to get the gospel out isn't free. That is why the Spirit of God wants to break down a fear for the area of finances, and a poverty mentality that can come upon Christians.

We are called to preach the gospel and to finance its preaching. The world will never help us and we cannot be dependent on it. But when believers see that their Father wants to bless them in every way, including their finances, they'll reach out for God's promises in this area and see Him do miracles.

This is no superficial, gold-pot-at-the-end-of-the-rainbow theology where everyone who believes right, rolls in luxury. That is nonsense. We say that God can and will bless us so abundantly that we have our needs met and enough over to give to every good work.

Most believers know about and are expecting a great, global end time revival. We have seen initial signs of these prophecies being fulfilled as evidenced in the fall of the Soviet Union and in what has happened in that land since. But as land after land ripens for the harvest, as doors for Christian TV open, when campaigns are possible in the Middle East, when invitations to preach come from Mecca, who's going to pay the bills then? The Body of Christ—the believers. Only those who have understood what the Bible teaches on God's financing and financial abundance and have received His willingness to bless others, will be able to do it.

A global, end-time awakening will come. James 5:7 speaks about it. It will, however, be the most costly revival in history. The Lord wants to prepare us so that we, independent of this world, have the means necessary to finance that revival. But clearly, those who teach it must reckon on jealousy and attacks. But it's better to know what God's Word says and come under fire than be a man-pleaser, impoverished, and never accomplish the work assigned us by the Lord—the Great Commission!

Something took place at that large collection in Uppsala in July 1987. Not only did much money flow in, but many were freed and stepped into a new liberty in the area of financial giving. To us, the offering was a great miracle. We were profoundly grateful to God and to all the loving givers. We began to realize increasingly that we were more than a local church. Our own description is apt: "We are a local church with a national responsibility and an international calling." As a church, we aim to reach all Uppsala with the gospel, but also all Sweden, Europe, Asia and wherever the Lord calls us.

A local church functions primarily through its members bringing the full tithe into the storehouse—the church itself. Our church boundaries were to be extented further, for when the work grew, we could see that the Lord wanted us to reach out far beyond the borders of our country. This is why it wasn't so extraordinary that He raised up intercessors and givers who lived elsewhere than Uppsala. We thank God for every intercessor and giver we have throughout Scandinavia and in many places around the world. Without their help we could never, and can never, do what we are doing.

Sometimes people think "I'll give my offering to a little work because a great work already has so much." That is rarely true. The opposite is so. The larger enterprise needs more money because it's larger, it's reaching further, is more effective, achieves greater results and is subject to more fierce attacks. We truly thank God for every giver who has faithfully supported us in everything the Lord has called us to do.

Following the opening of the new building, the work was really about to accelerate, but in 1987 we had no idea how dramatic and great it would be. Before I describe the next exciting aspect, I must, however, tell you about another emerging battle front: the Christian schools.

CHAPTER SEVEN

Christian Schools

To tell you about the complete cycle of events involving our Christian school I must go back to 1985. On May 28 of that year, we applied for a permit and the statutory educational grant needed to start a school. It was here that a long drawn-out, yet stimulating, battle began. The battle for the right to start Christians schools and the receiving of their rightful grants is not over yet.

The "seed thought" of starting a Christian school can be traced back to the beginnings of the church. From the start, besides a Sunday school, child-care center and a kindergarten, we envisioned a Christian school.

1985 was election year. We held the Faith Conference in a large Sports Stadium and about 4 000 people participated. One evening I preached using the Swedish blue flag with its golden cross as an illustration for my sermon about revival in the land. In my message, I said among other things, "What Sweden needs is a new government." I think I said it four times. Those words gave rise, of course, to a series of attacks on Word of Life, primarily from the left-wingers, the social democrats. For many years, left-wing Christians had pleaded for socialism. To question the socialistic government now and present alternatives was to go too far for some and it seemed more than many would tolerate. Why did I say it? And was it necessary to say it even if it was true? I am convinced it was necessary. Today, more than 10 years later, I hear many preachers quote those words. Not in biased tones, but with a rational insight into things as they are now.

Firstly, it wasn't a denunciation of social democrats generally, or individuals specifically. I have emphasized this several times. Secondly, it is fairly clear to everyone that communism, and its close cousin, social democracy, are documented, fundamentally non-Christian. To be sure, there are Christian social democrats just as there are non-Christian conservatives. The issue doesn't lie there but in the underlying ideology, its claims, its goals, and what it produces in a society.

It is not whether a social democratic government has done better or worse things. Nor is it what they have said at certain times or action they have taken concerning Christian values. Nor is it that other parties or ideologies are free from non-Christian elements and opinions.

Then what is the problem? The issue is over a long-term secularization of society. It is about an ideology which is contrary to Biblical Christianity, which in fact, they have attempted to replace. It is about a pretentious, totalitarian creed among the leaders, that wishes to develop a society reeducated into their own political ideology. It is about a government which after years in office, has thoroughly infiltrated the machinery of power, repressing every different opinion or idea. It is about an intolerance for anyone who dares not to conform; about government leaders who not only practice repressive measures, but who have set in motion a gradual indoctrination of the people. The result: Sweden has become one of the most effectively secularized lands in the West, deprived of most all Christian ideals.

Consequently, a new government was needed. Not because a conservative government would always prove to be much better or more Christian, but because in certain areas, at least, it held some fundamental values and followed another course, much closer to Christian morals and ethics.

It may seem as though expressions like "brotherhood," "unity" and "caring" automatically means that social democracy takes its inspiration from the Christian faith. But that is not so. In this chapter my focus will not be on social democracy, but on what really did happen when we started the Christian school... There was fierce opposition!

From where did the opposition arise? From the left wing social democrats! Nevertheless, it was overcome and that was something uniquely special and vital for our nation. It was essential that the typecast thinking of society should be changed. While the conservative wing showed much greater openness to private enterprise, and options, the reaction within the social democrat camp was totally rigid.

Our first meeting concerning the Christian school was with the Local Education Department in Uppsala. They were negative to the idea. We then went to the Regional Education Board. No, again. On to the National Board of Education, and another refusal. The question finally arrived on the Minister of Education's desk who met with us himself, surrounded by his dissenting advisers.

All this created problems, not only for us, but for the politicians. It was a headache for the left-wing majority to dismiss something which, in principle, they were forced to say yes to. They had to search high and low for reasons to stop the school.

Here, I believe, lies a prinicpal difference between conservatism and socialism. Conservatism finds it a lot easier to accept alternative views. (Even middle-of-the-road liberalism includes it in its fundamental idea.) It has always been generous towards those who think differently. In fact this is a part of Conservatism's view of democracy.

The idea of democracy in socialism is much weaker and more vague. Socialism defines democracy differently. Moreover it feels a moral need to regiment the entire society into its own ideological mold in order to create the socialistic state. When in power, left-wingers put their own people in the public offices more often than right-wing governments.

This became more and more apparent as we contacted these offices. What happened then? They formed their own committees and, looking back, we see that some of their conclusions are virtually hilarious. Firstly, their negative attitude (still the same today), was so conspicuous that it was sometimes embarrassing. In all fairness, not every case-investigator was the same. I must say, the Minister of Education began to treat us with far greater respect as time went on.

The subordinates however, were different. The chairman of the Local Education Committee, a social democrat, was positively unrelenting; Word of Life was not going to have a school! He was sure that the doctrines of Word of Life conflicted with the religious freedom in schools, actually meaning "freedom from religion." While the Local Education Committee was in session in August, Word of Life Christian School had started and wasn't thinking of stopping, no matter what they said. The Education Committee said "No," and gave as its reason the school's link with Word of Life church, whose founding deed states that our purpose is to promote Christian Bible teaching. Therefore the school couldn't possibly be "objective," in general subjects as is required by the National Compulsory School Curriculum.

First, this was strictly an assumption on their part. Second, the decision was in direct conflict with the European Convention guaranteeing human rights and liberties. Sweden's Compulsory School Curriculum (LGR 80) states explicitly: "public schools must make clear that human rights and liberties shall never be repressed using the laws of the countries." Yet this is exactly what they were doing! On this issue the word "democracy" was tested and "found wanting" by the left-wing majority.

Next, the Regional Education Board, came to inspect us and did a full-scale search. Everything was examined, then reexamined. Did they find anything? Yes. Among the absurd conclusions they drew one was this: "the pupils only studied countries whose flags included a cross." The children in one class had made models of the flags of our neighbouring Nordic lands and also happened to make the Swedish flag a little larger. "This," they added, "was discriminating." A junior class had drawn a map of the continents and forgotten to include the Antarctica. This, concluded the inspectors, proved that both teacher and pupils acted discriminatingly. They had excluded an entire continent! The inspectors' conclusions were as obnoxious and flabbergasting as they were spiteful. First and foremost they were aggravated by the school's connection with the church. We know how important this link is for both the financial and moral support of the school. We also know that this does not prove the school is unable to be objective, or unable to fulfil the requirements of the National Curriculum. Now we can see clearly that their objections were (and still are) about a socialistic aversion to private schools in general and Christian schools in particular.

Some journalists, accuse me of being negative towards social democracy. One certainly can have no confidence in an ideology when one sees its promoters in action and know what their real goals are. In a democratic society there should be enough respect for the individual to converse with him and the flexibility to change ones opinion when necessary.

The next stage was our dealings with the National Board of Education. Their opinions were divided. The lawyers were the most positive but the director was negative, so we got a refusal. Our visit with this Board was interesting. A lawyer, who said that he was not a believer, took out a State Church prayer book. Opening it to the Apostles' Creed, he started reading it just like in an old-time Swedish catechism hearing. He asked if we believed in the first, then the second and then the third article of faith. We answered "yes". Puzzled, he looked at the director, (a member of the evangelical Mission Covenant Church), and said that there was really nothing left to discuss.

The director, however, thought that was a bit too easy. Turning to us, the elderly lawyer suggested that the media attacks on us were probably because the State Church no longer really preached the Apostle's creed, and if they did, they would be as much the target of the press and public as we had been. The director said nothing, but afterwards, we got a refusal.

The next stage involved the national government. Maj-Kristin Svedlund, who is the administrator of our school, has done a magnificent pioneer job, greater than most realize. She and I were received by the Minister of Education who was visiting Uppsala at the time. Just that day, both Maj-Kristin and I happened to be very hoarse, and we wheezed and puffed our way through the interview. We who were accused of belonging to an odd healing sect that attacks the sick for being sick could hardly talk ourselves! It must have made a weird impression.

Principally, the minister asked one question. Did we believe the Bible's teaching on creation? When I answered "Yes," he had no further questions and we could leave. Some months earlier I'd been through similar "questioning" at the Regional Education Board by "frosty ladies" who distrustingly asked two questions. The first was about the Bible's account of creation and the second about the practice of homosexuality, do we consider it sin? Of course we said, yes.

The Bible's account of creation poses a direct threat to the theory of evolution which is woven into the fabric of our socialistic society. Certainly there is room within the framework of the Biblical narrative for various theories by natural science, and a school must present the alternative scientific theories. But this is not the underlying issue. In Sweden and the West, the theory of evolution has become much more than a scientific theory; it has become a "doctrine" of the society. In other words, it is used to justify the secular lifestyle. It asserts that man never fell or became sinful but that he is progressively getting better. He doesn't need the cross or Jesus as Redeemer. He is not in need of a helper, a saviour or a mediator, for God doesn't exist. Unfallen man needs no help to be cleansed, healed or restored. He has no sinful lusts, simply natural, animal instincts which must be lived out.

It is on this level, the moral plane, the clash comes. Here, we were hardly the dogmatic ones. It was both interesting and astonishing to see how biased people can be. What we experienced, was similar to the harassing of nonconformists in the Middle Ages. This time, however, it was the dechristianized, radical, socialistic cultural elite who sounded the decree of excommunication.

In the end, the government sent a one-man inspection committee, whose detailed investigation drew other conclusions than those before him. Among other things he pointed out that former investigations had gotten hung-up on my preaching more than objectively examining the competence of the school. He recommended approval and after many "coughs and hiccups", we got it on March 12, 1987. The Minister of Education should have the credit for this. He treated the school correctly and saw the wrongfulness of saying "no" to a school after the expert's recommendation for approval.

Behind the scenes though there was much mumbling and grumbling about the final investigator's findings. The mumbling is still heard today. It was "too positive" and didn't fit the very negative picture the mass media had painted. Nor did it suit the social democratic cultural idea or their school politics.

When the approval came, our joy was inexpressible. But the fight wasn't over yet. Next on the list was the statutory grant tax money specifically alotted for child education. This is a compulsory compensatory tax paid by us, designed to go to the students. The social democrats didn't want that. They meant that the funds should go to their public schools, not to the pupil, regradless of which ever school the child studied in.

Only when the conservatives came into power 1991 was there a change, a positive decision on grants. In the previous years Word of Life church paid the equivalent of several million dollars to keep the school going. Parents paid fees for their children, but these fell far short of covering the costs.

Today things are different and more fair. But it is healthy for parents, pupils and churches to go through tough pioneering times. We learn to call on God, to stand in faith, to work voluntarily and to invest our means in the future of our children. In a situation like ours one is exceedingly joyful and grateful to God to have a Christian school. It can absolutely not be taken for granted!

While all this was happening, the school grew from 34 pupils in grades 1 to 3 in 1985-86 to 550, spread in grades 1 to 9 in 1995-96. The administrator, teachers and staff have done a magnificent job in making it one of the largest independent schools in the country.

A school is always the scene of much intense work, and Christian schools are no exception. Nevertheless, the Christian faith as the basis of all teaching provides them with great stability. Sometimes we have been accused of shielding our children from reality. That is not true at all. Partly because reality is present daily in the mass media. Further, we have no intention of keeping the children isolated from society. The opposite is true. We give them qualified help to live in, and make a positive contribution to, the society around them. Other critics have vindictively asserted that all our students do is talk in tongues or suffer corporal punishment. Nonsense. Corporal punishment is nonexistent at school and prayer is made in the morning assemblies and in the private prayers of the pupils. On the other hand there is a harmonious, calm and peaceful environment which fosters good academic results.

Knowledge is important. Absence of knowledge creates prejudice. The mass media proves this repeatedly. But knowledge must be founded on a system of morals and students must be shown how to make right choices and to understand the true qualities in life. Consequently, we need Christian schools. Christianity came to Sweden long before secular, cultural radicalism. It was from Christianity that education and the schools of our nation arose. Universities were born from the Church's need to train priests and theologians. Elementary and lower secondary schools sprang from the need produced by the Reformation to teach people to read and write. They had to be able to read and understand the Bible themselves, not be tied to the expositions of the priests. Martin Luther and other reformers were devoted to the work of schools.

To assert that Christianity furthers prejudice is nonsense. On the contrary, secularization and dechristianization cause prejudice and ignorance to increase, brutality to spread, superstition and the occult to mushroom and the level of public education to sink. It is paramount that schools, Christian or non-Christian, contribute to the raising of the level of knowledge so that facts, not prejudices, objectivity, not opinions, form the lives and views of the people.

It is said that a Christian school will be limited, biassed, subjective and incompetent to create tolerant and broad-minded students. Not so! Through the firm foundation of the Christian faith, a personal relationship to Jesus Christ and a high level of scholarship, students become secure in themselves and mature enough to face their world responsibly.

We saw this clearly when we started Word of Life Christian High school in 1990. Possibly, it spread bigger shock waves than when we opened the elementary school, but it was an essential step. Today we have approximately 100 students and a highly qualified staff.

We knew that to have a High school was important, but now we see that it has been far more important than we realized. High school education is voluntary in Sweden. During the three years the students mature wonderfully. To see pupils leave High school after three years as mature and responsible young adults is a great joy. Much could be written about the High school but there isn't room here. I could describe the projects of the students, their independence, relationship to their teachers, chaplains and youth pastors, their study trips to different countries, their voluntary evangelism campaigns, spring fever in the third year with its finals, banquet, celebrations and a trip to Israel.

After much wrangling and a refusal from the socialistic Minister of Education, Göran Persson, (today, 1997, Sweden's Prime Minister) the High school finally received its official approval. It was the intervening conservative government that approved us August 12, 1993. Now, at last, we are pleased that our statutory grant has been awarded too. After a long battle and a meeting with the School Minister, Ylva Johansson, we finally got a "yes" in June 1996. This is largely due to one of the national daily papers taking our side and fighting for us in its main editorial!

In addition to this battle, we decided, after several years' anticipation and preparation, to start a university. September 1994 it started with 25 students in three faculties: Higher Biblical Studies (theology), a faculty for Philosophical Humanities and a Teacher's Training Institute. This was demanding but exciting. Step by step plans matured to meet the demands of university studies. Christian education on a university level was necessary in many fields. One, for example, was training for pastors. Two years at Bible School were important but not enough for language training, deeper Bible knowledge, theology, church and revival history and further pastoral subjects.

There was also a need for a Bachelor of Philosophy degree in history, humanities, political science and other subjects from a Christian viewpoint. The need of Christian journalists is immense. We need courses in media. We need Christian education for teachers for both Christian and public schools.

At the beginning the task felt enormous and we felt small. Little by little, however, everything has fallen into place and grown. The Lord has sent competent teachers who now give students first class courses of study. As time has gone on, we have come into contact with Oral Roberts University (ORU) in the U.S. This has led to a fruitful and significant collaboration, because it will make it possible for overseas students to study here.

CHAPTER EIGHT

Russia Inland Mission and Eastern Europe

In the autumn of 1971 I was walking past the castle in Uppsala on my way to the university library, when a sudden thought struck me: "One day, you will do a work in the Soviet Union, but not yet." I didn't think any more about it. At the time I didn't think it was from God, but the thought didn't leave me.

18 years later it became a reality. Of everything we have done at Word of Life, the work in Russia was surely the most intense, the most powerful and the most extraordinary. From the start of Word of Life we knew we would send out Bible school students "in victorious battle for the Lord." Accordingly, we laid plans for sending evangelism and mission teams through Sweden and overseas.

Several of our students had made journeys to the east previously. Among them were Ove Sandberg, Bengt Wedemalm and Michael Lundin. The assistant pastor in Södermalm church, Carl-Gustav Severin, had also been in the Soviet Union, first time 1985.

Carl-Gustav and I met regularly at the Wednesday night meetings I conducted at Södermalm Church and a warm friendship grew between us. As he told me about what was happening in the USSR I could feel the Lord drawing my heart there. Carl-Gustav asked me several times if I would accompany him but I felt it wasn't time. However, we prayed for him and the USSR because we wanted to help.

Soon we sensed it was time for our work to begin in the Soviet Union, and Carl-Gustav felt God linking his heart with ours. So a close collaboration developed and, in time, he and his family moved to Uppsala. Once there, he spearheaded the work, directing the combined forces of our members, preachers, finances and contacts with a far greater impact than if he'd been a one-man mission. Other churches joined forces and a unique joint-venture quickly developed.

Early in 1989 I went with Carl-Gustav to the Soviet Union for the first time. Together with Lester Sumrall and a company of preachers from the U.S.A, we visited Leningrad and Gattjina in Russia and Tallin in Estonia. It was a glorious time. On the way home I developed an excruciating pain in my ear—a counterattack from Satan because of the wonderful things that had happened.

One day, Carl-Gustav, Birgitta and I sat in our conference room praying and talking about the Soviet Union. While we talked, we felt the Lord was spurring us on to mission work in Russia and Eastern Europe in a greater way. After my trip to Leningrad, the Lord spoke to me and told me to invest 40 million Swedish crowns (5 million USD) to spread the gospel in the USSR. The truth was, we needed the money to pay off our new church building. Now, however, we felt that we must give priority to the work in the USSR. But how we were to go about it we did not know. The sum was colossal.

While we were talking, that afternoon, the "Russia Inland Mission" was born. The name came to us at that time and has never changed. Our assignment was to evangelize more than just the Baltic states and mega-cities of western Russia. We were to penetrate the interior and beyond, cross the Urals and go all the way across Siberia.

As we prayed, the presence of God came mightily among us. It was then I saw the vision. (I have seldom seen visions, but it happened then). I saw a train start out from Uppsala full of young people, Bibles, tapes, books, food and medicines. As the train rolled through central Russia, books flew out through the windows and the gospel was spread through the land. I took it to mean a "spiritual train". I thought it was an illustration of what the Lord wanted to do through us there. I had no idea it would be fulfilled literally,—that we would rent an actul train and spread the gospel along the whole Trans-Siberian railway.

We discussed how we would spread Bible teaching more effectively and decided to take up a collection for one hundred videomachines. During our Faith Conference 1989 these machines were "dedicated" to the service of God and then distributed throughout the USSR. (Some are still working today!) Wherever a videomachine was installed we sent teaching videos—and the Russians devoured them. Political change was coming to Russia, and while glasnost began to grow under Gorbachov's influence, churches began to spring up at the majority of these "video-outposts". We began to realize increasingly that our work had started at a strategic time. We'd jumped in at the first crack of the opening of the East. If we've ever done the right thing with the right people in the right place at the right time, we did then. When Russia and Eastern Europe opened, we were already in motion to spread the gospel.

Volumes could be written about this mission. The speed and success with which everything moved was miraculous. The Lord had given us a four year assignment and we worked as fast and as hard as we could and the work bore much fruit.

At the end of World War II a call had been made in the U.S. for 10 000 missionaries to go to Japan. Its people were disillusioned; they had lost faith in their ancient gods. However, few missionaries responded and, spiritually, Japan closed again, (though I believe it will reopen). We felt very strongly that if we did not obey God and invest all we had now, Russia would close in the same way. I am delighted we obeyed. I am also very grateful for all we've seen take place inside the Soviet Union.

Some good brothers at home thought I'd fled my responsibility in Sweden when they saw all the traveling and emphasis on Russia. But I could do it no other way. Today I am happy I didn't heed their admonitions to stay at home.

A period of feverish activity began. Carl-Gustav traveled non-stop! He's a wonderful brother with a big warm heart that beats for Russia—and the Russians love him. He has given his life to them.

More preachers and teams were sent in. Campaigns and conferences were held and step by step, new churches were started. In some meetings signs and wonders flowed down like rain from heaven. Many were healed from the most serious illnesses. After 70 years of inhuman tyranny under communism, the *"sun of righteousness had risen with healing in its wings"*. (Mal 4:2).

In January 1990 Carl-Gustav and I went to Donetsk in the Ukraine, then Moscow and finally Tartu in Estonia. The trip was important. It was an incomparable experience to see the hunger for God's Word in Estonia. When we distributed literature they almost pulled our arms out of their sockets to receive it. God did a great number of miracles in those meetings. Later I preached in a detention center for alcoholics in Moscow standing under a giant-size portrait of Lenin. Many came forward to receive salvation while the rats ran in the corridors. I had already felt a strong leaning towards Moscow, and later, it became a strategic center for us with its Bible school and dynamic, growing church.

Our last stop was Tartu. There we held meetings in a former KGB complex and prayed so loudly that the neighborhood around heard us. The meetings were powerful. Many were healed and met God in a powerful way. After the meetings were over and we'd gone, the Russians, who'd come from nearly every republic, refused to return home. Nothing was going to stop them from having more of this faith teaching, and they weren't going anywhere. Pastor Albert Turnpu was forced to start a Bible school then and there.

Today, many of those students have become preachers and pastors across Russia. Directly after the conference, several of them headed straight for the river, hacked holes in the ice and demanded baptism. Such was their hunger to follow Jesus. A sovereign, spiritual revival sprang from this event whose shock waves were felt across the USSR.

That same year we held a conference in Riga, Lettland. Thousands attended. On one occasion everyone went down on their knees and asked God for forgiveness for the sin of communism, renouncing it, while armed guards patrolled inside and outside the hall. Hundreds of people at the conference publicly renounced every form of anti-Semitism. It was tremendous to see the work of the Holy Spirit bringing people to contrition of heart, with sorrow and repentence.

All this time, the need for the printed word and teaching was becoming all the more pressing. Missionary Frank Arthur joined our publishing house and made a historic, pioneering effort, getting books translated, printed and distributed. A book can still preach when the preacher has gone home and in Russia every book was read by at least 15 people, and Bibles by even more. I thank God for the time he'd given me earlier to write several books on the basic elements of faith teaching. Those books now have proven very useful and have been translated and spread by the thousands. Now, over 4 million books have been printed and distributed in the East.

All the time we saw there was a great need, not only for faith teaching, but for the original, fundamental Christian doctrines. For several years I struggled to write the book "Doctrines" which was intended originally for Russian pastors. Russia had never had a reformation so their needs were infinite. What a joy it was when we were finally able to distribute them to more than 1 500 delegates at a conference for pastors and leaders in Moscow early in 1996.

The period between 1989 and 1991 was tremendously intensive. Great political upheavals were taking place at this time in the Soviet Union. Who would have believed that the entire iron curtain would collapse and fall so quickly! Yet the Lord had prophesied it several years before, and we knew it would happen!

In January 1991, as I sat watching the TV news I saw the Russian "black-beret" forces drive right over people in Vilnius, Lithuania's capital, and take the TV tower. On the screen I saw the parliament building surrounded. Chaos reigned. Suddenly I heard the voice of the Lord say, "Fly there now."

"Impossible," I thought. The reporter had just told us that some Swedish government officials had tried to enter but were refused visas. Immediately, I called Carl-Gustav and we agreed that we should phone our "friend" at the Russian embassy in Stockholm. Our "friend" was very interested in all we were doing in Russia and would have liked very much to visit our mission-headquarters in Uppsala. When we told him we needed visas to the Soviet Union, we got them immediately. In we went—but first we stopped in Leningrad to deliver a shipment of food. We had a couple of confrontations with some high-up Russian Orthodox priests in their communist limousines who'd stolen some of our supplies, then lied about it.

We arrived in Riga the day after the conflict over the government Home Office. Our contact in Riga told us how he'd stood on the barricades and preached Jesus to the people in the midst of the fight. We travelled on to Vilnius and found a city under total siege. In spite of that, the newly started church had hired the city's House of Culture and our meetings drew full houses. After one service I asked the pastor if it would be possible to meet Lithuania's president, Landsbergis. I had an inner assurance that the Lord wanted to strengthen him in the enormous pressure he was under while the Russians were doing everything in their power to stop Lithuania attaining its liberty. The pastor thought it was not likely to happen, but, his assistant knew someone who knew someone else, who knew someone else, who might be able to arrange it.

The following day we received a message that we would be given an audience with the president. The feeling was indescribable being allowed inside the parliament building after several security checks. The government officials had barricaded themselves and were living there day and night. Beds stood everywhere and Catholic pictures of Jesus hung on all the walls. On the roof a lone guard and his shot-gun kept watch. It wasn't much compared with the Russian tanks, loaded and ready to fire, lined up outside.

On the way up to the president's office as I passed the posters of Jesus, I suddenly realized these posters were an unuttered prayer for help. Once in the office, we spoke with president Landsbergis for 20 minutes. He and his wife looked haggard and worn out. They were under colossal pressure, standing alone against the aggresive might of the Soviet war-machine.

I felt I should say these words to the president: "Small lands have come out victorious against bigger lands, when they have turned to God. Assyria didn't succeed in defeating Judah when king Hezekiah turned to God." When I pointed out the posters of Jesus hanging all around indicating their belief in Him, he replied, "Yes, we believe in God!"

I reminded him how England and Churchill stood alone against Hitler's nazi Germany in the battle of Britain, yet managed to resist the onslaught. I also mentioned how the people in Philadelphia during the American revolution got nowhere with their constitution before Benjamin Franklin urged them all to pray. I said that if he and members of parliament would assemble for prayer, God would do a miracle and Lithunania would be free; I added that many Christians were praying for them the world over. The president stood up and looked happier, and I actually believe that the spirit of faith and a new strength came upon him. After a strong battle, Lithunania indeed miraculously won their freedom.

Some years later I was in Singapore when something remarkable happened. I met a pastor who was interested in Eastern Europe and I told him about our experience in Lithuania. Astonished, he stared at me and told me that during the crisis he'd felt the Lord urge him to call president Landsbergis in Lithuania but that he was never able to get through. He'd felt very frustrated for he knew he'd received the word from God. But he was both surprised and happy as I related to him how the Lord had told us to go in, how He had opened all the doors and provided us with the opportunity to encourage the president with a word from God.

Leaving Vilnius proved very eventful. First, our car ran out of fuel. We didn't make the last train in time and had to take a taxi with all our video cameras and other equipment. (Journalists were barred from entering or leaving Vilnius). At half past twelve at night we got stuck at a Russian military road block. When they opened our bags, we looked undeniably like journalists, and when we said we're "preachers," it didn't make matters any better!

Carl-Gustav tried bawling out the soldiers in German but it didn't work on them. I tried to improve the situation by saying "We have come with food for your people." But in my broken German it came out, "We have come to eat up your people." Happily the Mongolian guard was none the wiser anyway. He just looked sour and thumped the video-cases with the butt of his machine gun when we didn't get them open fast enough. My son Jonatan sat in the back seat keeping my private video camera out of sight. However, they even found that when they searched us. Half an hour later the man in charge came back having contacted the KGB. "Sorry" he said, and returned the cameras and videos and we could pass. We understood nothing, but thanked the Lord anyway!

Our taxi drivers had been so nervous that they'd handed out cigarettes to everything that moved non-stop, to keep the Russians from shooting us. Finally we were informed as to why everything had gone so well. The Russians had contacted the KGB who knew about our visas through our "friend" in Stockholm. They were informed that we had delivered a shipment of food to Leningrad, and that is why they were forced to let us go and why they hadn't dared to check our video recordings. It was certainly best for us, because the messages and prophecies of freedom and the visits to parliament recorded on them, would have incriminated us.

During our New Year Conference 1990-91 we invited a delegation of Russian youth for a visit. It was a powerful conference. Tagging along with them was a former KGB officer. He wasn't saved and was frightened by the intensity of the meetings. He had spoken to Carl-Gustav and then came to me. What he said almost made my jaw drop! He had a whole train for rent! A train! Having previously served as a propaganda vehicle for Komsomol, by the "Young Communists", he told us that the train was no longer in use, as communism was no longer popular. Could Word of Life use it, he wanted to know?

"Get that on paper, fast, before he changes his mind!" I ordered. And suddenly I knew, something fantastic was about to happen!

I'd seen a train in my vision but I never imaged it would be a literal train! But it was a real train! Things were put into motion fast. Two summers in a row this train rolled through the Russian interior just as I had seen in the vision. Full of young people, Bibles, Christian literature, tapes, videos, food and medicines, it took the message of Christ to the heart of Russia, from Leningrad in the west to Chabarovsk in the east. Stopping at every major station en route, the young people held meetings, dramas and shows, visited the local mayor, the hospital, schools, children's homes and a lot more besides.

Due to the huge evangelistic effort, today there are churches in nearly every town where the train stopped. While it rolled slowly along, some times at night on its journey, the young team opened the windows and threw books and Bible tracts out to the people running alongside to get hold of the Word of God.

The gospel now began to make inroads every-where. Missionary after missionary was sent in and our preachers criss-crossed the USSR proclaiming the Word of God from Magadan in the east, Irkutsk, Alma Ata, Kazakstan and Armenia in the south, to Siberia, the Urals, to Moscow and the "Golden Ring," to the Ukraine and White Russia and to the Baltic States.

Russians came from every region of the former USSR to our conferences which grew bigger and bigger. As time went on we felt the importance of concentrating on pastors' needs. Increasing numbers of young pastors were coming and it was wonderful to teach them the Word of God. Of the newly saved, some had been in prison, some had been in the maffia, others had been atheists.

These conferences for pastors proved very important. I've had the privilege of speaking to pastors around the world and of course, in Sweden too. But nothing compares with speaking to Russian pastors. These brothers have stolen my heart. I love to be with them. They're wonderful, kind, hungry and spiritually strong in the Lord. It has been indescribable to see them grow and to see how the Lord is using them. They are the future of Russia!

The republics then began to open up to us one by one, thanks to the labours of Carl-Gustav Severin. 12 000 people once came to a miracle meeting he held at Yerevan in Armenia. However, when we visited the same place later, there was pure bedlam. Orthodox priests stopped the meeting, fighting broke out and we were threatened with murder. However, things went well and despite fierce opposition the church in Yerevan has grown steadily since.

Azerbajdzjan opened shortly afterwards and Carl-Gustav took the opportunity to preach down by the Iranian border. In spite of muslim reaction, there is a church in Baku today also.

I could write volumes more: about the general who assisted us, about flying in the airplane belonging to the Minister of Defence, how we sang in the spirit in the Lenin museum, prison "cell groups", extraordinary miracles, Cossacks who tried to stop our meetings, plane crashes, etc. Russia is a wonderful land and it has been a wonderful time working there. Our Scandinavian preachers, missionaries, evangelists and volunteer workers have done a fantastic job! It is tremendous to see what can be achieved when each person finds his or her place and everyone pulls together. God never planned for a one-man band, or that one person should take or get all the praise for everything that is accomplished. It always takes a team and each one is equally important—and the glory is all the Lord's.

When Russia opened up, Eastern Europe opened too. The fall of the Berlin wall sent a wave of rejoicing round the world. This monstruous barrier had been the universal representation of tyranny and oppression itself. And God defeated the atheistic barbarity! Land after land in the east now opened up. Thanks to the efforts of Bengt Wedemalm and Mikael Lundin, we moved swiftly into Czeckoslovakia, (later to become the Czech republic and Slovakia), Hungary, Bulgaria, Yugoslavia and last but not least, Albania.

Albania, one of the last countries to relinquish communism, was a situation all to itself. In 1991, a unique door of opportunity opened to us—and a spiritual bomb exploded! Here is how it happened.

Scouting out the land, Bengt Wedemalm met the minister of culture. He was a democrat. The government had been forced, under pressure, to appoint some democrats into office during the time in which the president was still a hard-headed marxist.

When Bengt asked if we might rent the stadium he answered a straight "no." No Christian meeting had ever been held in Albania and the idea was unthinkable. But Bengt had another idea. He began to tell the minister about our church and choir, and about my book, "God, the State and the Individual", and suggested instead a "cultural-exchange program." On hearing our views about atheistic communism, the Culture Minister warmed appreciably, calculating that he could use it to knock communism and push his own party. We didn't favor a political party but he gave us access to the stadium and national TV on the condition that he should first hold a 10 minute speech on the virtues of democracy. We had no objections! Our skillful TV manager, Bo Sander, secured guarantees for the entire "culture-program" to be broadcasted nationwide on the state network. This was unheard of. Nothing like it had happened before. Albanian TV broadcasted four hours per night and we were promised two hours of them! Our TV manager Bo Sander piloted the project through many tricky waters.

Preparations got under way. Posters were put up throughout the capital city and everyone in Tirana knew that a big Christian culture-happening was coming up soon in the main stadium. Meanwhile, Carola Sögaard had won the Eurovision music contest and we invited her to accompany us.

On the night of the meeting, 20. 000 people filled the stadium. The atmosphere was charged with excitement. The Minister of Culture gave his speech while the people listened halfheartedly. Then the music started. A roar arose from the bleachers. The musicians played, Carola sang and I preached. The crowd got incredibly stirred up! It was impossible to talk to them more than a few minutes at a time, so we alternated with music and preaching. Gradually, the gospel began to make its mark. When I declared, "Atheism is dead," the crowd shouted its assent. Following up with, "Communism is dead!" they roared louder. And when I proclaimed "Jesus is risen from the dead," they let loose with everything they had.

A fierce battle was being fought in the Spirit in the stadium. My interpreter nearly fainted under the pressure. I had to almost carry him on and off the platform. Fights and skirmishes blazed here and there. Some people let off steam by setting fire to their T-shirts and waving them over their heads. Others threw themselves at the riot barriers, but when the time came to answer the call to salvation, the response was almost total. Of course, we don't know if everyone was saved, but we know that thousands prayed the sinner's prayer. We also know that that prayer went out live via TV and we still receive testimonies of what Jesus did that night in Albania.

It was a miraculous opening for the gospel into a land which had until recently outlawed even the mention of Jesus' name in prayer. Today we have an active nationwide mission program despite almost intolerable living conditions for our workers.

We have also started a farm project, so crucial in a land where farming methods are hardly better than medieval. Albania's isolation had been total. People's minds had been almost destroyed with all the severe brain washing and propaganda. But Jesus knows how to open a country, and He can open a nation in a day.

Our mission into Bulgaria is another hair-raising story. The land was in a critical situation and needed insulin desperately. In a snowstorm we flew insulin and other medical supplies to Bulgaria in our private airplane and met the president and prime minister. In connection with this visit we held meetings in Plovdiv and Sofia, meetings which were accompanied by mighty miracles so that the deaf heard and people with defective vision were healed.

Following up these meetings in 1992, we rented the main arena in Sofia and the Palace of Culture. Preparing well and calling the campaign, "Heavenly Explosion" we presented the gospel clearly and had it broadcast live on Bulgarian TV from the Palace of Culture. This was the first Christian TV program ever aired in the nation. The day after, more than 40 000 came to the outdoor arena and many, many were healed.

But it was more than the Orthodox church could tolerate. On our return a year later, the communists had regained power—though under another name—and in collaboration with the Orthodox church, labelled us a "sect" and I was declared "persona non grata", a person not welcome, in Bulgaria.

The plane we had chartered stood for several hours at Sofia airport while an anti-terrorist force with hoods pulled down barred our 140 member team from leaving the plane.

Curt Lahti, the team leader, attempting to negotiate from the steps, heard one of the soldiers whisper in his ear, "I'm sorry I have to do this,"—he had been saved the year before in the campaign! While this was going on, I attempted to enter the country via Thessalonica. However, the border station was informed. My name was black listed and no amount of talking helped. So I went to Athens and waited there. At the same time, Bengt Wedemalm, already in Sofia, conducted the meetings, and strangely enough, nobody bothered him. In fact, during one service, healing miracles rained down from heaven and many were saved.

While waiting at Athens I read the following verses from 1 Thessalonians 2:17 and 3:1-13, especially 3:1-2: *"So when we could stand it no longer, we thought it best to be left by ourselves in Athens. We sent Timothy who is our brother and God's fellow-worker in spreading the gospel of Christ."*

Bengt phoned and reported the victories gained in Sofia and the tumult at the airport. He told us that the American embassy had sent a report to Washington about the outrage committed by the Bulgarian government.

I'm still not welcome in Bulgaria, but the day will come when I will be. Meanwhile, the work there has grown steadily. We have helped the churches start a Bible school and we held conferences, all under constant opposition from the government and persistent harassment of some Christians in the very worst communist style. But the Helsinki committee is now turning the eyes of the EU onto Bulgaria's extremely undemocratic methods. The Bulgarian Christians are full of confidence and are continuing to overcome in Christ.

Not having been allowed to enter Bulgaria, our team flew on to Athens and held a campaign there. It was a special happening. We rented The Rex, a private theatre where the Orthodox church was powerless to stop us holding meetings. They tried, nonetheless, by shrieking in megaphones on the street outside. But The Rex was packed and many were both saved and healed. The event was broadcasted on Greek TV via TBN (Trinity Broadcasting Network) which has stations in Greece. This paved the way for us to later broadcast five times a week on TV throughout Greece—this has proven to be a very fruitful ministry.

Another campaign held in the summer of 1992 was unusual. Renting a ship on the Danube, we filled it with a large team and followed its course, starting in Vienna and stopping in towns along the way—including Bratislava, Budapest and Belgrade. We preached the gospel in every city, distributed literature and prayed for revival in the various lands. The most dramatic of all was entering Serbia and preaching the gospel in Belgrade which was under boycott by the United Nations. The stadium was filled just the same and many were saved. A terrible oppression hung over the city, aggravated by a hatred of foreigners because of the UN boycott. Still, people listened attentively to the gospel of Jesus who can transform the heart of man and turn hatred to love. It was glorious to see people come out for prayer. We felt Jesus' love for these people and how He cares for everyone on both sides of the various borders and how He desires to help all of them..

And so the entire east opened up for the gospel. In many ways it was like Russia. Churches were established in country after country. Campaigns were held, teams and preachers were sent in and books were translated. In addition we helped to start eight Bible schools and supplied them with teachers and materials. Several of these were in churches we had earlier helped to start in Russia and eastern Europe.

The Bible school in Moscow is something extra-ordinary. Today it has over 500 students (1996) and is run by Word of Life church in Moscow. The Bible school in Brno in the Czech republic is run by Word of Life church there and is attended by 350 students. Many of the students are from other countries including Bulgaria. Since the government had closed our Bible school in Sofia, students from Bulgaria come to Brno.

Laboring faithfully alongside the evangelistic campaigns, our TV ministry has played a signicant role in the mission work. We began broadcasting in a small way on local TV in 1988, but the growing missions in eastern Europe presented us with multiple media opportunities including those occasions when the meetings were broadcast live in Tirana, Sofia and Prague. In St. Petersburg 70 million viewers could see the special program from the Sports Palace. We also broadcast on several local stations across Russia. Russian TV came to Sweden and made a series of outstanding documentaries about our church.

So the four years passed and over 40 million Swedish crowns came in for the spreading of the gospel in the former U.S.S.R. After that, God gave us a 2 year extension. This extension had to do with the Russian

Jews. Now that there are established, growing works, we still feel we have but begun to obey the Great Commission. We have only just begun to spread the gospel of our Lord Jesus Christ.

CHAPTER NINE

Israel and Operation Jabotinsky

Every born again Christian has a special place for Israel in their heart. Poor theology, prejudice or ignorance can stifle it but it is there just the same. It should not seem strange, because without the Jewish people western civilization wouldn't be where it is today. Where would we be without Moses, Isaiah, Jeremiah, Samuel, David and Solomon? What would we be without Jesus who came from the tiny tribe of Judah but died for the sins of a whole world? Anyone who has felt that Calvary-love flowing towards him cannot but thank God for the people through whom it came. Jesus himself says to the woman at the well of Sychar *"...salvation is from the Jews"*. (John 4:22).

When we started Word of Life many people mentioned the importance of Israel to us but I felt that the time wasn't ripe for specific action. We had to focus on establishing the church, building up the Bible school, and organizing the Christian elementary school. However, when we had finished all of these, and opened our new facilities in 1987, Israel opened to us also. Dr. Lester Sumrall arranged a trip in the autumn and we took 100 people with us. It was a significant trip for many reasons. In the plane on the way there, before I had set my foot on Israeli soil, the Spirit of the Lord said to me, "I am taking you to Israel where I will let you bypass every religious organization and get you high up, and you will be known as a friend of the Jews." It was difficult to even imagine, but a few years down the road it proved to be just as God had said.

Modern Israel is a miracle. Jews are arriving there from every corner of the globe to settle in the land God gave their ancestors as an everlasting inheritance (Gen 13:14-17). Not only is it a land with a great past where you can see the ancient sites—monuments to people and events in Bible times—it is a land where God is active today. But more important than both these is the fact that Israel is the focal point of God's future events. The Messiah will not return to a large western city, He will come to Jerusalem.

So we started taking groups to Israel, and it was wonderful. Since 1987 thousands of people, most of them Bible school students, have joined us on 25 trips there. To visit Israel is to see the Bible through new eyes. The land comes alive. Israel's geography is like a fifth gospel—a visual aid to the previous four. I was overtaken by an insatiable desire to learn everything about Israel and the Jewish people—their history, archaeology, geography, politics, religion, lifestyle and traditions. Understanding the Jews can never be treated like a sideline attraction or just one topic among multitudes of others. Getting to know about Israel is a serious life-and-death matter, one of vital importance to every believer.

On examining Israel's history one is struck by the recurrence of a particular phenomenon—anti-Semitism. The causes have always been fear, prejudice, aversion to foreigners, ignorance, superstition, twisted theology, misquotes from the Bible and hard hearts. The nominal, institutional Church has been guilty of gross anti-Semitism from both a theological and biological standpoint. Theologically, because the Jews belong to another religion that does not acknowledge Jesus as Messiah; biologically because they are different race of people. The sufferings and persecutions of the Jews throughout history have been hideous, the most incomprehensible being when six million were killed in the concentration camps of the Second World War. In addition, their persecutions and distresses through the centuries have been the worst in the sphere of Christian culture.

Our excursions to Israel have given us many lasting valuable experiences. It is wonderful to preach in Jerusalem on the themes of the church, the prophetic ministry of Jesus and His future return to the mount of Olives. It is a privilege to tell of His miracles in Galilee where He fed the 5 000 and walked on the sea. It's exhilarating to repeat the Great Commission that He gave and to preach about the time the first gentiles were baptized in the Spirit by the Cesarean coast.

At the same time, it has been stimulating to get to know modern Jews, whether they are religious or secularized, political or non-political alike. The more time you spend in Israel, the more you understand its way of life and begin to perceive its future significance. The eyes of the nations are turning increasingly towards this tiny nation whose surface area is no more than the size of the state of New Jersey in the U.S.

As time went on, the need for teaching about Israel became increasingly apparent. First, we must inform people of the Biblical promises concerning the people, the land and its future. Christians who are positive towards Israel are often foggy about her right to her own territory. They haven't seen that God really promised the Jews this tiny piece of land forever. But when they realize it, Christians are under obligation to put things right and to denounce and start opposing anti-Semitism wherever they find it. There is a pressing need for this in Russia and the former eastern bloc. It has been marvellous to see formerly anti-Semitic Russians experience a complete turn around and begin to fight for the rights of Israel.

This change is essential also in Sweden, western Europe and the rest of the world. Some Christians have been duped by superficial and slanted reports on Israel by the secular press. Others have been fooled by substitutional theology—a poor brand of Bible interpretation that attempts to do away with the Jews although the Bible never does. Paul says in Romans 11:1: *"I ask then: Did God reject his people? By no means!"*

For a period of time we helped several Russian Jews who had left the Soviet Union for Israel and traveled through Sweden on the way. Our church had the privilege of caring for them for a few days. We began to realize increasingly that we must help the Russian Jews home. The Bible says clearly that

God will regather His scattered people to the land of Israel. Ezekiel 36:24-28 makes this clear: *"I will gather you from all the countries and bring you back into your own land..."* Verse 28 continues. *"You will live in the land I gave your forefathers; you will be my people, and I will be your God."*

Since the founding of the State of Israel in 1948, and even long before that, Jews have been making their way home. Today, we see them arriving in Israel from every part of the globe. The Bible, however, specifically mentions another exodus from "the land of the north." The Word of God informs us that this will be an exceptional and far more extensive return than the exodus from Egypt. Jeremiah 16:14-16 says: *"...the days are coming, declares the Lord, when men will no longer say, 'As surely as the Lord lives, who brought the Israelites up out of Egypt,' but they will say, 'As surely as the Lord lives, who brought the Israelites up out of the land of the north and out of all the countries where he had banished them. For I will restore them to the land I gave their forefathers.'"*

We have seen this begin to take place just like the prophecy said. Through the fall of communism in the Soviet Union, the way opened for the Russian Jews to return home. It was an open "window," an opportunity, but for how long?

When the four years of our commission in Russia were completed, the Lord gave us a two-year extension, this time, with a focus on the Russian Jews. Through our trips to Israel, many Russians had become aware of the importance of blessing the Jewish nation and people, as it says in Genesis 12:3, *"I will bless those who bless you and whoever curses you I will curse...*"

On these trips we have always scheduled a specific study day featuring special speakers such as Harry Hurwitz, (former adviser to prime ministers Menachem Begin and Yitzhak Shamir), Jan Willem van der Hoeven of the International Christian Embassy in Jerusalem and others like them. Their expertise and experience have done much to open the eyes of believers to the plight of the Jewish people and the nation of Israel. Many have started helping the Jews and opposing anti-Semitism.

A network of pastors now began to take shape in Russia. These leaders displayed a wholly new attitude towards Israel and were eager to bless and help the Russian Jews.

At home in Sweden we were in touch with the then orthodox rabbi in Stockholm, Aron Katz, who introduced us to David "Dudu" Fisher. Dudu is a widely acclaimed Jewish tenor. Throughout the world, irrespective of their politics or religious fervour, Jews love him.

Dudu came to hold a concert for us at Word of Life—and got the shock of his life! He wasn't used to Christians and had never met so many who loved Israel so fervently. A warm friendship grew from his visit.

In 1991, we arranged two important journeys to Israel. The first was an excursion for business people in February. The Gulf War broke out just then but we went anyway. The Lord had given us a word from Judges 18:6, *"Go in peace. Your journey has the Lord's approval."* We were the only group of tourists traveling around the country at the time—to the great surprise and delight of many Israelis. Lines weren't long to the various attractions either. At the nearly deserted Ben Gurion airport we were handed gasmasks and injection syringes in case of a gas attack. No one knew at the time if Saddam Hussein had gas or bacteriological warheads on the Scud-missiles he was launching against Israel.

At nights we had to rush off to the air-raid shelters every time the sirens wailed signalling incoming Scuds. My son Benjamin was with us. He was excited! And in Jerusalem we felt safe. Saddam would hardly risk the wrath of the Muslim world by sending a missile right into the Omar mosque! Tel Aviv, on the other hand, suffered several hits.

We left Israel the same day the war was over. It was the feast of Purim, that celebrates the victory of the Jews over Haman in the book of Esther. Today's Haman, Saddam Hussein, had launched 39 missiles at Israel, yet only one person died as the result of a direct hit. A miracle! It was magnificent to see how the Israelis cared for each other and stuck together as a family. It was wonderful to be there and pray for the land's protection.

Tourism was slow after the war, so when we arrived in June with 900 people, there was great jubilation and much publicity in Israel. We met the Prime minister and had an unforgettable evening at the Sultan's Pool open-air theatre where we invited Israelis to a celebration night of song, dance and speeches. The mayor of Jerusalem, Teddy Kollek, was there as was Shlomo Hillel.

In 1993 we took a contingent of Russian pastors to Israel. Many had not been outside their country before and it was a delight to see them completely 'devour' Israel. What they saw there was not what their old communist propaganda had sold them. They were astonished by Israel's abundance of delicacies and fruit! Some of them had never seen a banana or an orange. They ate and laughed, and laughed and ate! Our Jewish guide, also Russian, could hardly believe her eyes. She never believed that Russians could be happy, open, loving and positive towards Jews. But this was a new generation of Russians!

In Tiberias I preached to them about the historic responsibility of the Russian people to bless and help the Jews. It was then that a word from the Lord came to us. "Get the Russian Jews out of the Soviet Union!" The interest and involvement had been there years before but now the assignment had been given, and Operation Jabotinsky was born. On the Word of God and at this specific command, we began to organize ourselves for work with the Russian Jews. We began instructional and information sessions with the Russian churches and met Jewish leaders in Russia. We visited synagogues and culture-centers. We put on "culture-nights" with Israeli songs and dances and gave information on the best ways to get to Israel from Russia.

In the midst of all this, I just happened to mention in one of our services in Uppsala, that we needed a ship to enhance the operation. In our Bible school at the time were two students, Mr and Mrs Langaker. It just so happened that Mr Langaker was owner and captain of a ship, and he asked if we would like to borrow it. Later, in November 1993, he donated M/S Restoration to Word of Life! The ship, a W.W. II troop transport ship from the American marines lay in

Seattle, Washington, U.S.A. and was in need of renovation and repair.

Here begins the story of an 18-month long miracle in which the Lord sent help in every way until everything was shipshape. And, what a change! Only those who worked on each detail from the start know the wonders the Lord performed. Thirty Scandinavian volunteers moved to Seattle working endlessly together with American friends, removing layers of rust that had accumulated from years of lying at anchor. It was transformed into a shining commissionable vessel in blue and white. It was glorious to smash a bottle of olive oil against her bow as M/S Restoration was commissioned for service. She set off for Sweden and arrived on Yom Kippur, the Jewish day of atonement. After some additional repairs, she left Sweden for Russia on Easter Sunday 15 April 1995.

During this time we had received help from Christians everywhere. They saw Operation Jabotinsky as a faith project and committed their lives and time to equip and commission an entire ship. Others gave their time to develop a network in Russia and set up routines for the Russian Jews to wind up their lives there and make their way to the harbor where M/S Restoration was waiting. It took a series of miracles before the "maiden voyage" on 24 June 1995—and yet the operation had hardly begun.

While M/S Restoration lay in the Seattle harbor, I was visiting the U.S.A. There I met Dudu Fisher, who was singing on Broadway. When I told him about the vessel and how we'd got it, he burst out, "This must be God!" To my question about what he was doing to help his people home—and would he like to come to

Russia and sing in concert, while I spoke? he answered, "Yes, let's sing them home!" And so we arranged a tour via Sweden where Dudu sang at Word of Life in Uppsala followed by the "Circus" in Stockholm and then Moscow and St Petersburg.

The concerts in Russia were fantastic. Many Jews came. It felt apocalyptic as I presented them with this unique opportunity for them to go home to Israel. The words gripped them and Dudu's singing heightened the atmosphere. Later, we met passengers on the ship who had attended the concerts and had made up their minds then and there to go home to Israel.

Shlomo Hillel is another delightful friend. He is a Labour politician, has been the speaker in the Knesset and is the chairman of the United Israel Appeal, Keren Hayesod. We met Shlomo when our church was helping Russian Jews in the early days. Shlomo was visiting Sweden and was deeply affected when he saw the way Birgitta, my wife, who is not Jewish, stood on the wharf receiving Russian Jews. It impressed him so deeply that he has mentioned it several times since. Shlomo himself was involved in Operation Babylon in which 150 000 Jews were smuggled out of Iraq between 1948 and 1951. It was good to meet him and have his support and encouragement, especially in the early days when Jewish Agency didn't have a clue as to what we were doing.

Jewish Agency, responsible for almost every Jew who returns to Israel, mostly uses airplanes and in the beginning they were not at all favorable towards our ship. They were troubled that they didn't quite have us under their control. That was true, they didn't. They also thought the ship appeared old fashioned and so on. It has, however, proven to be an out-standing vehicle for transporting Russian Jews home to Israel. While on the ship, they have time to wind down, think over their situation and prepare themselves for their new homeland. They can take much more luggage and have a whole lot more fellowship. Talking with Shlomo Hillel and others, however, we obtained the support we needed in dealing with Israeli organisations and authorities. Their prime concern, in the end, was that Russian Jews were getting home, and how they got there was only secondary.

This was amply illustrated when we succeeded in rescuing 25 Abkhazian Jews from an almost impossible situation. Just prior to this incident, one of Jewish Agency's men had commented, a little conceitedly, that they wouldn't be needing our ship. Later, several Jews were found stuck in Abkhazia which was at war with Georgia after its attempted breakaway. The border with Russia was closed and these Jews could neither get to Tbilisi, Georgia's capital, nor cross the border to Russia because their passports were invalid. The only way to get them out was by ship. We had the ship! When we rescued them after an exciting and risky operation, the local Jewish Agency said to us, "You have succeeded where we could not!"

It was wonderful to be able to do it. More Abkhazian Jews are now waiting for our ship to return there. From those who we rescued, we heard that they had cried to God and prayed that the rescue vessel would come. One man even told us that an angel had visited him and promised that he would be freed and get to Israel.

We are only in the initial stages of Operation
Jabotinsky. As we were refurbishing the ship the
Lord told us that the first three years were preparation for what would come later. So we haven't rushed
ahead, many parts of the puzzle must first be in
place. Still, it has been fantastic to sense the Spirit of
God leading us and supporting us in this operation,
and only the future will reveal how important it really
is.

One of our contacts and friends in Israel is Harry
Hurwitz. He and his wife have visited us in Uppsala
several times and we always meet when we are in
Israel. Mr Hurwitz, is a walking encyclopedia on
modern Israeli history and politics while also a meek
and very dedicated and astute man. It's fascinating to
hear him tell of Israel's origins, the development of
Zionism and Israel's problems and visions. How
refreshing to hear facts other than those selected by
the news media. The closer we get to the return of
the Messiah, the more important it is for every
believer to understand the place of Israel on God's
agenda.

After the Holocaust of the second World War the
opportunity finally came for the Jewish people to
return to their own newborn nation of Israel. This
was 1948. Since then, anti-Semitism has changed
identity. Now it's called anti-Zionism. While some
people say that Jews may set up their homes in certain smaller tracts of the old British mandate, Pal-
estine, there is no doubt that the surrounding Arab
nations would like to get rid of Israel altogether.
Groups of Muslim activists work for the dissolution
of Israel either by political pressure, propaganda or
military force.

Many Christians have been unaware of what has gone on in the Middle East and have not fully realized the importance of blessing Israel. Their "evangelical-church" thinking has said that if the Israelis aren't saved then neither should they be supported. They haven't understood God's plan to restore them: that He is bringing them back both to their land and Himself. With Israel's birth, the prophetic fulfillment for the words of Psalm 102:13 has come: *"You will arise and have compassion on Zion; the appointed time has come."*

Yes, the time has come to drive out all so called "theological" anti-Semitism, and to accept the Bible's view of the Jewish people, who are the root of the olive tree which supports the branches (Rom 11:17-18).

Yes, the time has come to stand up for Israel, to understand the times in which we live and what will happen in the future.

Yes, the hour has come to quickly and effectively take the opportunity while there is time, to rescue as many Jews as possible from the former Soviet Union.

Yes, the time has come to see God do abundant miracles and to restore His people Israel.

For this reason we want to reach out with Operation Jabotinsky, while there is time.

CHAPTER TEN

Looking Expectantly to the Future

There is no limit to what God can do through a church that fully obeys Him. The Lord has always chosen to work through His body—i.e. through local churches. This will be increasingly important as time goes on. In the first three chapters of Revelation, we see the Lord speaking to the different local churches. There His plans are revealed and there, too, is the power to accomplish them.

One can never be a "private Christian". Each man is not an island unto himself. We need each other in the entire Body of Christ, and most of all, we need each other in the local church. The gospel has sometimes been preached as though it were a happy pill; something that exists just to make me happy. This is deceptive and leads nowhere. Every believer must become part of something bigger than himself and be of service there. That something is the church. This is the way God's kingdom is spread.

It has been fascinating to watch our church grow and spread during each particular intensive period.

No church is perfect, including ours. But it is not by finding fault with the church that people become spiritually great. It is by doing something about these shortcomings. We have many wonderful members who have seen this and thrown themselves into the work of the church with a faithful, servant-like attitude. The Bible comments of Issachar in Gen 49:14-15 and this can be said of faithful people: Issachar is a strong donkey lying at rest in his paddock. And he saw how good is his resting place and how pleasant is his land. Then he bent his shoulder to the burden and submitted to labor (Swedish Bible 1917 translation).

We have very many genuine servants in our church. Some made great personal sacrifices for the work to advance.

When we were under the most intensive onslaughts, I suffered to see how some members were treated. Some were bullied at work, others were denied employment or lost their jobs because they belonged to Word of Life. Even children were harassed and families were ridiculed and isolated. Yet they stood firm for Jesus, and God granted us unity and steady growth.

So it was a huge victory when, on May 30, 1990, we were scheduled to broadcast a Sunday service on Swedish TV—nationwide. But what a reaction from the newspapers! Many of them wanted to stop the morning service—if it would have been possible. The uproar only increased interest, and by the time of the broadcast, people were "on tip-toe" throughout the country. The evening papers must have been thinking backwards, for they advertised loudly for us as Sunday drew near.

The service was a total success, and despite the storm, it helped change the Swedish people's attitude towards us. Those who ridiculed us said: "Your services are not like what we saw on TV," but they really are, and many realized it.

Another TV-show that proved beneficial to us was Göran Skytte's interview with me. Publicity around the show was great. My time with Göran Skytte was very interesting. I was sligthly amused at our common past in the left-wing-hippie movement. Göran was a very able reporter and smart enough not to attack me on the flimsy evidence of hearsay only. The interview took an hour, an intensive hour, but I think he got answers to most of his questions, and some things to think about for the future. I received a lot of response from people who'd seen the show. What is more, I heard later that it was taped for use by universities for training students in rhetoric because, they said, I had used every rule in the book! I was not aware of this during the interview. I've never studied oratory. Nor have I ever attended any "charm courses" in the U.S. as some have accused me of!

By degrees, attitudes toward us have changed. And as I said earlier, we have changed too. Everything that grows changes. Our beginning with a hundred members, mostly young people, cannot be compared with what we have now. We now have a church of over 2 000, and thousands of visitors from all over the world.

Let me say a few words about leadership. There is a big difference between being a "dictator" and operating in authority. To start a great work and then build it, implies a lot of responsibility. Leader-

145

ship is not just being boss. It is about shouldering responsibility practically, financially and pastorally and not running when it's not going your way. Leadership is to be faithful until the work is done. I've sometimes had a sneaky feeling that some of those who were irritated with me for "making most of the decisions," would rather have liked to be boss themselves.

We actually have many leaders in our church. I have sometimes thought, "If only my critics realized how little I actually make decisions for all that's constantly happening around here." We make up a great, cooperative team, and the leaders have extensive areas of responsibility.

This whole question of authority is an interesting one. I cannot go into more detail here, but there is a lack of leadership in many countries today. We've worked so hard on pulling down all authority that didn't suite us that in the end we only have our own, confused, judgement to rely on. We have become our own authorities. In the modern western world, man has set himself up as his own god. But we are very inferior gods and can't save a flea!

A pastor and a Christian leader is a servant. He doesn't have more authority than that which Jesus gives him, the Word instructs him and his church acknowledges. The Lord can, however, give the most imperfect pastor, (whose heart longs to serve Him) a great boldness and authority under Jesus and His Word and the guidance of the Spirit. It is most important that the Body of Christ rediscovers true, spiritual authority, its extent and its limits. This is especially true in a world that has cast nearly all authority overboard. Otherwise the risk is great that Christians will become isolated and divided and anarchy will reign.

Another event that changed the spiritual climate in Sweden was Korean pastor Yonggi Cho's visit to Stockholm in 1994. I was invited by pastor Stanley Sjöberg, to speak at a seminar for business persons and to interpret for Yonggi Cho.

Two things happened. One was that I was invited by Yonggi Cho to speak at his church in Seoul, Korea, which in turn, resulted in my being asked to become a board member of his organization for church growth. The other was that I met and heard Sverre Larsson, a great Pentecostal leader in Sweden. Sverre was the speaker before me at the seminar in Stockholm. When he was through, he came and greeted me warmly. The people there rejoiced and a photo of us together was printed in the papers. This became an opening between the Pentecostal movement and Word of Life

Later, Sverre came to preach at Word of Life. Our church warmly received him and the news of the meeting spread throughout the nation. Denominational barriers gradually opened bit by bit, and relationships, especially with the Pentecostal movement, were normalized.

This is what the Lord wants, of course, and He has used Sverre Larsson in a special way to do it. It has also led to an open, honest and loving fellowship between us for which I am very happy. It was all so unexpected, but very genuinely from God who loves His children whatever camp they are in.

Growth implies a lot of change and if we look ahead we can see much change yet to come. It will be very exciting to see what the Lord will do in Sweden and throughout the world.

At the time of this writing, the Lord has opened new and exciting doors for us. One of the most thrilling is the new Christian TV channel, Christian Channel Europe, (CCE). The Lord promised us a media explosion and it has finally begun. We are broadcasting Christian TV across all of Europe. We have received testimonies of healings and salvation from many countries. Even muslims in north Africa have responded and want to know more about Jesus. To have Christian TV across the entire continent of Europe is a unique breakthrough and the beginning of a dramatic rewriting of the spiritual map in Europe.

Our church doesn't claim to have the only revival in Sweden, but we work as though we were alone, we shoulder our full responsibility, fully aware that we are absolutely not the only ones around. God is using a lot of people in a lot of circles. We should not allow ourselves to be caught up with exclusiveness or pride, neither should we bow and scrape in false humility, waiting for something to happen. There is a godly balance in the life of joyful, courageous, loving faith. We all want to mature in this.

I have many times been criticized and presented in a negative fashion in both the Christian and the secular press. That picture has been wrong. On the other hand, those who respect me and look to me for leadership, sometimes have put me on a pedestal, as though there couldn't be revival in Sweden without me and Word of Life. This is also wrong. We all have our place to fill. I sometimes get the feeling that some people think that we shouldn't have a place at all, or that we do too much or get too much publicity. In all these things we must maintain a sober and sound view of ourselves and do what we feel the Lord is telling us to do. I believe that it is very important that we know each other's hearts. The greatest desire of my heart is to love Jesus and to willingly serve Him. I love Him and am infinitely grateful to Him that He saved me. And, He saved me so that I could serve Him.

But when I attempt to obey Jesus, I do not want other people to be injured. With all my heart I want to serve our church, but also the whole Body of Christ, in whatever measure I can. I want to and I must tell about what God has given us. This is the way the Body of Christ becomes more closely knit together and the gospel is spread to as many as possible.

I believe we are in a very exciting phase of development in Sweden and in Europe as a whole. The gospel is arousing interest again and many people, especially the young, are getting saved and coming to know Jesus. Across Europe there are many signs that indicate that the younger generation is searching for God again.

The spiritual climate in Sweden is changing to the degree that it could lead to a countrywide revival. That is something that God really wants. There are multitudes of young people who have never seriously heard the gospel. They must hear the genuine gospel confirmed by the power of God. God is a good God and in His love He wants to reach out to every person on earth. I am convinced that He will soon do just that to thousands here in the Nordic countries. The result will be a transformed Scandinavia and

thousands of these northerners will be equipped by
God to go into all the world with the gospel. Scandinavia is a region that has long had a mission calling
from the Lord.

When a person is saved, a desire begins to arise
within him to serve God. It brings great joy and satisfaction to serve Him. Jesus says in John's gospel
4:32, 34, *"I have food to eat that you know nothing
about...My food,"* said Jesus, *"is to do the will of him
who sent me and to finish his work."* Service for God is
food for the inner man and the highest satisfaction
anyone can ever attain. To hear the word of the Lord
is a great privilege. To follow Jesus and to do His will,
to see God do miracles and His will accomplished,
nothing can be of more value than this. This is something God has for everyone! He has it for you and He
wants you to experience this joy and satisfaction.

Your life need not be a failure. You don't need to
live an empty, meaningless life. Jesus wants to fill
you with His peace and joy and give you a real reason for living. You can step into something far
greater and exciting than you ever imagined. Why?
Because Jesus loves you and gave His life for you
when He died for you on the cross. There He shed
His blood for you! He died in your place. He took
your sins on Himself, and by believing and receiving what He has done for you, you can have a brand
new life. You can become a child of God and His
working partner. He will change you by His grace
and your life will become something wonderful
and beautiful. A holy adventure is waiting for you
when you give your life to Jesus. He loves you and
has many wonderful things in store for you. God
bless you!

Postscript

This book is not the place for a comprehensive coverage of the doctrines we preach at Word of Life. There are many questions you may have. For answers to these, may I refer you to my book *Doctrines—The Foundations of the Christian Faith* where I cover most doctrinal points. For further study, may I recommend *The Church of the Living God*, *God the State and the Individual*, *A Life of Victory* and *Faith that Overcomes the World*.

Books by Ulf Ekman

A Life of Victory
The guidance, help and inspiration you need to put God's Word first. Fifty-four chapters, each dealing with a particular area of the believer's life. *288 pages.*

The Apostolic Ministry
How do we recognise an Apostle? What role does the Apostle have? What can we learn from the life of Paul, the greatest Apostle? Ulf Ekman gives Biblical guidance in this book. *128 pages.*

The Authority in the Name of Jesus
When you receive a revelation of what the name of Jesus really means, you will have boldness like never before. *Booklet, 32 pages.*

The Church of the Living God
The Church of the Living God is something far beyond what we think or experience. It is the place where the End-time Revival will have its source and climax—and you have a place in that Church. *158 pages.*

Destined for Victory
God has victorious plans for you. His plans never fail! In this book you will discover: I How to aviod fear of failure I How to withstand the attacks of Satan I How spiritual laws operate and I How Gods Word always brings results. *Booklet, 32 pages.*

Destroy the Works of the Devil
Jesus came to earth to destroy the works of the devil. His death on the cross struck Satan a death blow. Jesus triumphed over him and won the victory for YOU! *Booklet, 32 pages.*

Doctrine—The Foundations of the Christian Faith
Ulf Ekman gives an objective and biblical account of each fundamental doctrine of the Christian faith. In days when the Christian message is increasingly diluted and twisted *Doctrine* will be an asset for every pastor, leader and believer. *256 pages.*

Faith that Overcomes the World
Explains how faith arises, how it becomes operational, and what makes it grow. *144 pages.*

Financial Freedom
A thorough, biblical study on money, riches and material possessions. *128 pages.*

God is a Good God
God has given you abundantly more than you can ever grasp for your entire lifetime. This book examines God's character and nature, and reveals His overflowing love for you. *Booklet, 32 pages.*

God, the State and the Individual
God not only deals with individuals, but with nations and governments. You can change the destiny of your nation! *112 pages.*

God Wants to Heal Everyone
Discover the wonderful fact that God's will is to heal everyone—including you. *Booklet, 32 pages.*

The Holy Spirit
The Holy Spirit is your guide, your teacher, your counselor and your helper. Discover how you can live each day in the power of the Holy Spirit. *Booklet, 32 pages.*

I Found my Destiny
Follow Ulf Ekman from his boyhood home in Gothenburg to "Livets Ord" – Word of Life Church in Uppsala, Sweden. From 1983 until today Word of Life has become a center for education, evangelism, mission and reformation in Sweden and throughout the world. *150 pages.*

Jesus Died for You
Blessing is a daily reality when you understand the power of the cross:
I Satan's plans were crushed I Sickness was defeated I Poverty was broken I Depression turned to joy. *Booklet, 32 pages.*

The Jews—People of the Future
Clarifies basic truths about the people and the land. Historical facts and biblical prophecies combine to reveal the fulfillment of God's End-time Plan. *160 pages.*

The Power in the New Creation
A new dimension of victorious living awaits you. The Lord is with you, Mighty Warrior! *Booklet, 32 pages.*

Prayer Changes Nations
Ulf Ekman teaches here on what characterizes the time before revival, the work that needs to be done and how the Holy Spirit can change every believer into a bold prayer-warrior. *156 pages.*

The Prophetic Ministry
"Provides essential guideposts for the operation of the prophetic ministry today." From the Foreword by Demos Shakarian. *224 pages.*

Available from your local Christian bookstore, or order direct from the publisher:

Sweden: Word of Life Publications
P.O. Box 17, S-751 03, Uppsala, Sweden. Telephone +46 18 16 14 00
Fax +46 18 69 31 90. E-mail order@livetsord.se

Australia: Ulf Ekman Ministries
P.O. Box 2324 Mansfield Qld. 4122. Telephone/fax +61 73 849 53 25

UK: Word of Life Sweden
P.O. Box 70, Edenbridge, Kent TN8 5ZG UK. Telephone +44 1732 867 171
Fax +44 1732 867 111

USA: Ulf Ekman Ministries
P.O. Box 700717, Tulsa, OK 74170, USA. Telephone +1 918 488 0881
Fax +1 918 488 0906 Toll free # 1 800 428 1760.
E-mail uem@compuserve.com

Canada: Ulf Ekman Ministries
P.O. Box 66058 Heritage Postal Outlet, Edmonton, Alberta, T6J 6T4 Canada.
Telephone +1 403 887 3313 Fax +1 403 887 3355.
E-mail ulfekman@hotmail.com

✂ WORD OF LIFE

The Vision that God gave for the work at Word of Life, Uppsala, Sweden is:

Equip my people with My word of faith
Show them their spiritual weapons
Teach them how to use them, and
Send them out into victorious battle for the Lord!

☐ Yes, I would like to receive Word of Life Newsletter free of charge
☐ Yes, I would like to receive information about Word of Life Bibleschool
☐ Yes, I would like to receive Word of Life Product Catalogue.

If you want to know more about Word of Life, fill in this form, send it to us, and we will supply you with further information free of charge.

Name:

Address:

State: Country

Zip Code: Telephone:

Word of Life, P.O. Box 17, S-751 03 Uppsala, Sweden.
Telephone +46 18 16 14 00, Fax +46 18 69 31 90 E-mail info@livetsord.se

---

Place
Stamp
Here

Word of Life
P.O.Box 17
S-751 03
Uppsala
Sweden